CARRIE,

WISHING you & your
CLUB MEMBERSHIP
SUCCESS!

GABE

THE
DEFINITIVE
GUIDE TO
MEMBERSHIP
MARKETING

Gabriel Aluisy

Edited by Shirley Jump
Jacket design by Gabriel Aluisy & Richard Jibaja
Interior design by Justine Parks

Library of Congress Control Number: 2017901638
ISBN: 978-0-9905832-3-3
10 9 8 7 6 5 4 3 2 1

1. Business & Economics 2. Advertising & Promotion
First Edition

Published by Shake Creative
http://shaketampa.com

Printed in the United States of America

THE DEFINITIVE
GUIDE TO
MEMBERSHIP
MARKETING

SHAKE PRESS

For Lucas & Marco
Nothing is Impossible

TABLE OF CONTENTS

FOREWORD

BY RICK COYNE & GREGG PATTERSON

This book is not about magic elixirs or silver bullets. It's about logic, reality and the psychology of sales. It is about strategy and planning to reach your market's relevancies and sound techniques to increasing sales closing ratios.

Soon after immersing himself into the world of private clubs Gabe realized that sales and marketing were key to the club's financial stability. He also learned quickly that sales and marketing of private clubs was a disturbingly misunderstood process. This book takes a step by step approach and is a perfect primer for Boards, Membership Committees, General Managers and Marketing Directors. There are incredible lessons for the entire team.

Gabe writes very similarly to how he speaks. His message takes a natural progression leading to logical and understandable conclusions. From sales strategies to the building of a winning team, to social media and networking, virtually every area of the private club marketing opportunity is touched in this guide book to membership.

Combined with proper market due diligence and intelligence on what your members and potential members want and need, virtually every private club can realize greater potential for increased growth, retention, member usage and member satisfaction.

If you subscribe to and implement the principles described within this book you will most definitely transform yourself and your team into more proficient salespeople and marketers.

As the late Robert Dedman Sr. once said, *"With members everything is possible! Without members, nothing is possible."* Philosophically, this is the perfect book to get all of your key players on board with the reality of a changed culture and the means to penetrate an ever changing marketplace. Read it and pass it along. It will make a difference in your entire organization.

Rick Coyne
CEO, Professional Club Marketing Association
Managing Partner, Club Mark Partners
Lifetime Achievement Award Winner – BoardRoom Magazine
2 Time Gary Player Black Knight Award Winner
rcoyne@clubmark.com

Everyone who's in business wants to sell their "stuff" to people who are hungry for the "stuff" they're selling. Creating, packaging, communicating and selling the "right stuff" to the "right people" requires marketing. And to the innocent, marketing is simple and uncomplicated---find out what they want, then give it to them.

But for those of us who manage clubs, who are in the business of creating, packaging, communicating and selling "the club experience", We Who Do know how tough real world club marketing can be. The devil is in the details. And We Who Do need help "spanking the devil."

We club managers are looking for a Club Marketing Primer that'll give us background into the complex world of club marketing, a document that'll provide insight into the club buying community, a "mentor" to guide our creative process, a document that'll explain how to properly package the goods, services, programs and facilities we've created, how to communicate those packages to the right audience and how to secure a commitment to buy from those we've targeted.

Many of us "out here" in the real world are needy---and lost.

Then along comes a writer who knows marketing, knows clubs and knows how to explain the complex ins and outs of the marketing cycle to those of us who are hungry---but clueless.

That somebody is Gabe Aluisy who's been "in the marketing trenches", knows his stuff and has written the definitive guide to membership marketing---called, not so surprisingly, "The Definitive Guide to Membership Marketing." Better than anyone I know who's "attacked" membership marketing, Gabe breaks The Marketing Adventure into its component pieces, explains all those bits and pieces in language non-specialists understand, provides a "template for action" and does it all in an upbeat, "can do", positive way that gives confidence to those of us who are hungry for insight into The Marketing Journey.

Gabe's book walks the reader through The Marketing Cycle. Membership marketing defined---done. Changes in the wants, needs and expectations of the user community---done. Changes in the way memberships are being marketed---done. Data collection and interpretation---done. Tools club marketers need to generate and deliver the message---done. Channels of communication to be understood and used---done. To sum up "The Definitive Guide to Membership Marketing"---Gabe "done good."

Gabe hits it all. Clearly and succinctly.

If you're in the club business, you need Gabe's book. It'll give you understanding. It'll give you process. And it'll deliver a coherent vision of The Marketing Journey.

Buy it. Read it. Use it. And give thanks to Gabe for giving us---"The Innocents"--- clarity and understanding.

Gregg Patterson
President and CEO
"Tribal Magic!!!"
Creators of WOW---Builders of Community

ACKNOWLEDGEMENTS

First and foremost I want to thank my wife, Ana Maria Aluisy, for her help and support as I wrote this book. Without her, my thoughts would not have made it to this page. Next I'd like to thank my good friend Chris Krimitsos, who lit a fire in me to get this book written and who has mentored me along my journey as a speaker and podcast host. I'd like to thank Gary Teaney, Ronica Richardson, and Adam DiMuzio, who pushed me to carve out my direction and have advised me on my path. Many thanks to Alex Rodriguez and Doyle Buehler, who held me accountable and encouraged me as I wrote this book. My sincerest gratitude to Topher Morrison and the team at Entrevo USA, whose business accelerator has opened doors I never thought were possible. To my father, for instilling a passion for the game of golf in me. To all my friends and family who have voiced their support, thank you!

INTRODUCTION

Marketing has been a dirty word in the private club industry for a long time. I'm intent on disproving that notion. Marketing doesn't have to be sleazy or unseemly and it shouldn't conjure up images of used car salesmen, heavy handed approaches, or the sale of the minute. In fact, much of marketing, what I would call good marketing, isn't even selling. It is much more subtle than that. It's not discounting either. Good marketing will actually help you raise your perceived value in the mind of the public.

This book is the missing guide they never handed you when you took that role as general manager, membership director or membership committee member. It's the down-in-the-trenches lessons that they didn't teach in your college marketing courses. It's the stuff they don't cover at industry conferences.

In the first section of this book I'll describe the current state of our industry and how we got here. I'm also going to show you why I believe that most clubs are approaching their membership wrong, why they're focused on the wrong things and why they're going about it in the wrong way. And don't worry, I'll be providing you and your club a solution to each of these.

As you progress further into the book, I'm going to equip you with the tools to modernize your marketing efforts. In this book you're going to learn what marketing channels you have available to you right now and how to maximize their uses in growing your membership. I'm even going to share some up and coming marketing channels and tactics that you should know about and start utilizing today. You'll find out what statistics and key performance indicators you should be tracking to ensure you're hitting your goals. I'll also give you some little known hacks for things like building an email list from LinkedIn, negotiating better deals with vendors and getting quoted in major publications.

Finally, towards the end of the book, I'm going to lay out my vision for the future and tell you what you should be prepared for in the next ten years and beyond. I'll share with you where I see clubs and membership marketing going and hopefully get you thinking about the ways you can set yourself up for the future.

My goal in writing this book was to share my strategy and the lessons I've learned from the wins *and* the losses. I've tried just about everything you can imagine both in my own businesses and in the ones I consult. Some things worked and some didn't. I've stood on the mountaintop with my arms raised high and fallen flat on my face just as many times. I'm sharing these tools with you because

I want you to learn from my successes and my failures so that you'll have you a leg up on your competition and be on the right path to membership success.

So what got me interested in working with private club membership? Well, I'm the son of a former PGA club professional. My dad put a golf club in my hands at the age of three and I've had a passion for the game ever since. I was an anomaly growing up in Baltimore, Maryland and playing the game. The city of Baltimore is not a mecca for golf and none of my friends played or were interested in golf. That is, until a guy named Tiger Woods burst onto the scene in the second half of the 90's. Once my friends caught the golfing bug they all took jobs at private golf clubs. They were caddies, bag boys, shoe cleaners and even assistant pros. I spent a lot of time at the exclusive clubs in and around Baltimore in the late 90's and early 2000's thanks to my friends. We played a lot of golf, mostly on Mondays, and I always dreamed of becoming a member of a club someday.

The first private club I ever joined was on a remote island in the eastern Pacific back in 2008. I had been in the workforce grinding it out since the minute I stepped out of college and I wanted to escape my routine for a while. I wanted to break away from the rat race I felt I was in and immerse myself in a new culture on another continent. I decided that I would live on a 30 mile wide speck on the map called the island of Siquijor in the Philippines. My uncle lived there and my best friend Matt was willing to join me. But by the middle of the summer, both my uncle and Matt had gone back to Baltimore to attend to personal matters. This left me all alone in a grass hut in a third world country. It was the first time I'd ever felt truly by myself.

Far from my home and a foreigner in a strange place I began to seek out things to do to pass the time. Luckily, the Filipino people were an incredibly inviting and welcoming bunch. Having always loved sports, I began to play a lot of basketball at the public court. One day while playing, I met some guys who asked me if I liked tennis, and I told them I did. They invited me to the town's only private club, aptly named the Siquijor Tennis Club.

After playing a few times with them, I decided I would like to spend more time there so I joined. The club had a whopping initiation fee of what equated to $20 USD. It was the best twenty bucks I ever spent.

I spent every morning and evening for months at the club, which consisted of one clay court and a small building. The club employed only one person, who opened the club to line the court, was the ball boy at matches and locked the gates at night. Because the club only had one court, doubles was the most common game. I loved it there and playing tennis every day had me in the best shape of my life.

The guys would often drink beers, smoke and cast wagers as they watched other members play and I was one in particular that people paid attention to. I was the first Caucasian member in the club's history, and as such I was something of a spectacle. I wasn't very good at the time, only a 3.5 level player, but crowds would watch anytime I was on the court. I often chuckle at the irony of the white guy being the odd man out at a private club. I got good playing there though, and by the time I left I was a 4.0 player thanks to a lot of pointers from the members.

I had some amazing meals at the club too. Now, when I say amazing, it was for entirely different reasons than we'd have at our local clubs here in the United States. They once had a potluck seafood buffet with sea snake as the main attraction. Another time, the firemen brought over ribs. As I was enjoying one, they asked me, "So how do you like dog?" I tried not to gag as I smiled and nodded my head.

My days spent at the club were relaxing and filled with interesting conversations with warm and welcoming people. Some of them became like family to me. These folks showed me the power of community. They helped alleviate that alone feeling.

Today I'm a member at a country club in Tampa called Carrollwood Country Club. It has 1,200 members, 27 holes, 12 Har-Tru tennis courts, a resort style pool, gym, bocce ball courts, restaurants and bars and everything else you would expect from a fine private club in the United States. But you know what? At its core, it gives me the same things as that little club in Siquijor. It's camaraderie, community, competition and a place where I can be myself. I need that club and they need me. It's a special relationship I know that I won't find in any other place.

Gregg Patterson, the famous former club manager of The Beach Club in Southern California, says that those of us in the private club industry are "on a mission from God." He's absolutely right. Our private clubs are one of the last vestiges of a society that has become cold, impersonal and even dangerous. It's a haven that the world needs to escape to and it's our job to make sure it survives for generations to come.

When I got back to the United States and got back on my feet, I started up a design and marketing business. Naturally, I was drawn to golf and private clubs. I began to work with them almost immediately. Today I have the pleasure of working with and speaking to clubs all across the country. I'm able to interview the brightest minds in our industry on my show, Private Club Radio. It's an honor and a passion of mine and I'm so happy that you've also found this as your calling. My sincere hope is that we can move this industry forward and take it to new heights together.

1

CHAPTER ONE

HOW MEMBERSHIP MARKETING HAS CHANGED

For hundreds of years, private clubs sustained themselves on an elegantly efficient and uncomplicated system of membership: the member referral. This is affectionately referred to as "the good ol' days" or the "heyday" of the industry by members and staff alike. People of like minds came together and invited others that shared their status, education, profession, worldview and, most importantly, their passions. Their common passion for golf was often at the heart of these groups.

As the end of the 20th century drew near, a big shift occurred. In the 1990s, reports came out from industry organizations saying that the demand for golf was increasing dramatically. To keep up with demand, experts were saying we would need to build one golf course every day. Later in that decade a guy named Tiger Woods appeared on the scene and drove interest and participation in the sport to new heights. By the turn of the millennia, clubs were popping up left and right, flooding the market. With it the first fatal flaw of the club industry, oversupply, was born.

The second major mitigating factor to the change that clubs have undergone was the economic downturn of 2008. During this Great Recession, which was not limited to the United States but truly a worldwide disruption, discretionary spending declined. To put it plainly, golf, tennis and other activities that private clubs had to offer quickly became luxuries that many just couldn't afford. Sure there was plenty of insulated wealth, but folks in the middle and below opted for less expensive entertainment options. Things like video games boomed because they were cheap and more easily accessible than sports that took months and even years to learn.

The third, and for me, most impactful, disruption was the result of the boom in the information age itself. People became immersed with access to new entertainment options right at their fingertips. As a result, the world sped up dramatically. Things like on-demand television and music streaming have created an insatiable appetite for instant gratification. Golf on the other hand is a four-hour commitment. Five if you want to do a little practicing beforehand. Six if you want to have drinks with your buddies afterwards. To many, this was incompatible with the direction their lives were moving.

With the emergence of social networks, the emotional bonds that were once steadfastly the domain of private clubs and similar institutions, were replaced nearly overnight. All of a sudden, people could make connections and share experiences with those sharing similar interests across the globe. They didn't have to meet for a match or commiserate over a cocktails, they could play games together online, share photos and geek out over their hobbies in message boards.

The onset of mobile devices changed the game further. Communication has become effectively limitless. Now we can work, find and maintain relationships, order our goods and services, access an endless library of media and learn everything we need to know about any subject without picking our heads up off a pillow or couch cushion. It's amazing and scary all at the same time.

THE MILLENNIAL DISRUPTION

At the same time this shift took place a new generation has emerged that is wholly unlike any that has come before. This group has been referred to as Generation Y or simply as the Millennials. These are people who would have hit their adulthood right around the turn of the millennium, hence the name. They are currently the largest generation, outmatching even the baby boomers. At the time of the writing of this book in 2017, they are aged 20-36. They have a current spending power of 4.4 trillion U.S. dollars and as little as 10 years will make up 75% of the workforce. For these reasons, this is not a generation that can be ignored by our industry any longer.

After careful observation and research from countless sociologists, psychologists and business people, there are some commonalities, shared value systems and personality traits that can be identified within this group, which I'll describe for you below. While I know there is no one size fits all approach when it comes to dealing with people, the

3

following characteristics are meant to provide you with a shortcut that will help you communicate to this generation in as effective a manner as possible.

It's also important to note that even though many of these trends have been spearheaded by the millennials, you'll find they are pervasive in our society from top to bottom. This is really a cultural shift with far-reaching implications blurring the generational gaps. The key traits I'll describe are not solely the domain of the millennials anymore. You'll see these same characteristics springing up in all groups, from Baby boomers to Gen X'ers.

I'm incredibly bullish on millennials and their place in the private club world. I think clubs have all the right ingredients to satisfy the desires of this generation. Clubs only need to recognize those desires, and make them a focus. Hopefully, I can show you a few ways to do that at your club.

EXPERIENCES NOT THINGS

The first and most important thing to realize about this generation is that their value system is unlike those of the generations who have come before. Millennials value the experiential over the physical world. They would sooner splurge on a ticket to a music festival than they would buy a shiny new Corvette. Many would prefer travel and adventure to luxury items like purses and watches.

Millennials place value on access over ownership. Who needs to own when you can rent and have all the fun with none of the headaches and maintenance? The emergence of Uber, the ridesharing service, and Airbnb, the room sharing service, highlight this fact.

The wonderful thing is that private clubs are all about experiences. If you think about it, every round of golf that someone plays is a new experience. You'll never hit the same sequence of shots twice. You'll never find yourself in the same place on the course from one round to another. That's what keeps us coming back. Club programming is very often centered around experience as well. Things like wine tastings, casino nights, live entertainment and the like are all based in the experiential. These can all be marketed in a way that would be extremely appealing to millennials.

FAMILY FIRST

The next most important thing to realize about Generation Y is that this is, by and large, a family oriented group. Millennials aren't the type to join an old boys club like their father's generation. You know the one I'm talking about, right? That old club where the good ol' boys sit around drinking scotch, smoking their cigars, playing golf and hosting the weekly poker game. Yeah, that doesn't happen much with this bunch.

Millennials are looking for places to take their kids. Both the husbands and wives are likely to have careers so the time they spend with their kids is precious to them. Beyond that, large purchasing decisions are often made or at least advised on by the ladies in millennial households. That means your club better have some options geared towards women, and your marketing needs to show it if you want to have the best chance at success.

5

Don't be afraid to put couples in your collateral materials like brochures and membership packets. Make sure to post photos of the ladies' groups on your social media pages. In fact, make sure to use social media networks that women prefer, such as Pinterest and Instagram. Have conversations on your social networks about women's issues. Doing these types of things will make your club more attractive to this generation.

VALUE VALUES

The next characteristic of the millennial mindset is the deep value system this generation holds. Brands that have put their values front and center have been rewarded time and again. The most notable example that comes to mind is TOMS, the shoe company. When TOMS burst on the scene in 2006 with their "one for one" program, giving away a pair of shoes to the underprivileged around the world for every one sold, the brand caught fire.

It's crucially important to keep your club's values front and center in your marketing efforts and on your website and social media accounts. Let people know what you stand for. Whether you have started a recycling program, use environmentally friendly pesticides and cleaners or your club has created a fundraiser around a cause like cancer, tell that story to your local community.

Another point of differentiation I've seen clubs make is in their farm-to-table approach. Many clubs have started a garden on their property and are using the vegetables and herbs they grow there in the food that's served in the restaurants. Don't be discouraged if you're a city club. You don't need to have a ton of space to create a garden environment. Just follow the lead of the Jonathan Club who built an herb garden on their rooftop.

I recently visited The Westmoor Club on the island of Nantucket. That club has its own charter fishing vessel that takes members and guests out into the Atlantic. Some of the day's catch is brought right back to the kitchen so the members can enjoy a fresh caught seafood meal. Another club, Goodwood in the United Kingdom, has even placed a honey bee farm on their property. With bee populations dwindling, this is both delightfully novel and an act of sustainability too!

Most likely your club does some real good in the community or for the environment. If by chance you don't, it's time to start thinking of ways you can. Start small. Not only will you begin to attract a new type of member, your existing members and your staff will take even more pride in their own club.

Miles Tucker, General Manager of Hillcrest Country Club outside of L.A., related a story to me on Private Club Radio about this very thing. At his club the kitchen staff helped build a garden, and planted and harvested the vegetables that would be served. For nine months there was zero-percent turnover in that kitchen, a feat you rarely hear about. That's the power of becoming a more conscious club.

SOCIAL PROOF AND THE AGE OF INFLUENCE

Social proof is not a new concept, but with the advent of the internet and the speed at which information is disseminated, the influence of social proof has dramatically shifted. At its essence, social proof is simply a testimonial. It's one person telling another person how good or bad a product or service is. Today however, it's not just one to one, it's one to many.

It used to be word of mouth was the only social proof people had. Today our younger generations rely on sites like Yelp, Google Places, and Angie's List to help them decide what products and services they'll buy. These sites efficiently signal to potential prospects whether they should proceed or not. So it's massively important that your club manage its reputation online.

Beyond the review sites, social proof happens on sites like Facebook, Twitter and Instagram. This is often a squandered opportunity by clubs. So often I see private clubs focus their social media efforts on tournament results, or weather reports or their membership specials. That stuff is all fine and good to sprinkle in occasionally, but they are missing the point of what social media is all about: conversations and connection.

It's 10 times more powerful to have someone else tell your story or do the selling for you. I encourage clubs I consult with to have their members, guest and even staff write compelling testimonials about their club experience. Let others be the voice of the brand and create a narrative. This is a much richer experience that people can connect with.

People don't want to be sold on social media. They don't want to be updated on things they're not a part of. They want to hear stories and connect, and they want to discover new things. Event photos and tournament results are not engaging. Save that stuff for your member newsletter. If you want to reach millennials and win on social media, be authentic and let others praise you in front of their networks.

Take a look at Chapter Six for even more in-depth ideas on how to maximize your social media strategy.

DISRUPTING THE OLD MODEL

So can clubs survive this assault from technology and from this cultural shift? Can they reinvent themselves and stay relevant in an increasingly crowded marketplace vying for people's discretionary funds? I think they can. However, I think there has to be a major shift in membership recruitment tactics for it to happen.

The first thing you have to do in order to move forward is to realize that those good ol' days are gone, and they aren't coming back. That doesn't have to be lamented either. There's a bright future for clubs who adjust not only their programming but their outreach into the local community and beyond. I hope to share some theories, lessons and tactics with you in this book that will set you and your club on a course for success.

For me there are three key areas that are holding most clubs back when it comes to their membership marketing efforts.

- Their membership sales process is fundamentally flawed

- They are communicating the wrong message

- They are ignoring what works for nearly every other business model out there

In the next section, I'm going to show you how I think you can change all that and dramatically increase the effectiveness of your membership marketing efforts. You'll have to decide if it's the right approach for your club, but if nothing else hopefully I'll get you thinking about and challenging the status quo. Maybe it will spark something you never expected or thought of. Maybe it will cause you to tweak your process even in the slightest way. If that happens, I've done my job.

NOTES:

CHAPTER TWO

MEMBERSHIP IS NOT A SPRINT

When it comes to private club membership, sales are not a sprint. Most people will agree with that simple and trite statement. You've probably heard it before from a board member or even a general manager. The problem is, the advice that comes next is often wrong, too. The classic follow up to "it's not a sprint," is usually "it's a marathon." I'm going to show you why it's not a marathon either. In fact, effective membership sales are actually a series of short sprints, more like a relay. Just like a relay, you need to have a strong team from beginning to end and you need to maximize every leg of the race.

The overwhelming majority of private club marketing directors I've met treat the sales process like a sprint. Here's the classic scenario I've seen played out over and over. The prospective member is referred to the club or finds the club through some marketing channel. The membership director schedules a tour and in about an hour will briskly shuffle them from one area of the club to another. They'll probably hop in a golf cart and see a few holes, stop by the pool or fitness facility, have a peek at the tennis courts, tour the dining rooms and banquet facilities and arrive back at the clubhouse and in the MD's office. The prospect will then be handed some pamphlets about the club and talk numbers. The savvy membership director will ask for the sale because that's what they've been trained to do at some point in their career. After all, good salespeople ask for the close, right?

The problem is, that tried and true membership sales process isn't working like it used to. But why is it getting harder and harder to sell a private club membership? I've heard a number of theories posed from industry experts who talk about more competition, changing value systems, time-constraints, aging populations and so on. All of those have some truth to them. But I think there's something right under our noses that's even more important to recognize and it has to do with the methodology of *how* we're selling.

A few months back I had the pleasure of speaking with Susan Greene on my show, *Private Club Radio*. Susan is the current PCMA President and membership director at The Oaks Club near Sarasota, Florida. If you have the pleasure of meeting Susan, you'll be instantly struck by her bubbly personality and bright floral outfits. She's a Florida gal, after all. But beyond her famously welcoming personality lies a very sharp salesperson. She's keenly aware of her market and the strengths and selling points of her offering. Suffice it to say, if she got you in a room for an hour she could sell you just about anything. However, instead of sharing her tips for getting a prospect to put pen to paper, she made a statement that caught me by surprise. "Your goal as a membership director shouldn't be to make the sale, it should be to move the sale forward," she told me.

I'd love to tell you how when that line hit me, the clouds parted and the trumpets sounded. Except it didn't happen that way at all. In fact, I said something mundane like, "Great advice, Susan," and moved on to my next question in the interview. In the days and weeks that transpired I let that statement marinate. I knew this simple truth had something profound behind it, but I didn't know how it all fit in just yet. It took me talking to psychologists to figure out why it was so important.

KEY CONCEPTS FOR A DISRUPTIVE IDEA

I regularly chat with psychologists. Not to clear my head or work through a deep-seated issue, but to pick their brains on my marketing ideas. You see, I firmly believe if we can understand how our market thinks and how they will instinctively react, we can better position ourselves for optimal results. Who better than a psychologist to tell us what our prospects are thinking?

During one of these conversations I focused my questioning around creating desires. What does it take to create a desire in the mind of a consumer? The discussion naturally wove its way through a number of concepts, but eventually landed on the notion of habit formation. It made a lot of sense to me. We desire things for which we have built a habit. Conversely, habits can be built by associating experiences or things with a desirable outcome. It's a simple concept and it was my first key.

It only takes a quick glance at modern technology success stories to realize why habit forming behavior is the Holy Grail for brands. The very mobile device in your pocket or purse right now is the best evidence I can present. Surveys have shown that nearly a third of folks would prefer to give up sex before they gave up their mobile device. Why is this? Because our phones have become our biggest habit. Everything that is contained in them has been designed with habit formation in mind. Every time you see a little red circle around one of your apps it's a trigger that leads to a behavior. You see the notification icon, you want to press the button, you get rewarded with something. Maybe it's an important email, maybe it's a cute picture of your friend's baby on Facebook, or maybe it's the next episode of that podcast you're really into.

Nir Eyal's brilliant book, *Hooked: How to Build Habit Forming Products*, explains the process of how habits are formed with our everyday tech. It's a four-step process of triggers, actions, variable rewards and investment. Using our example above, that little icon on your phone's screen is the trigger. That trigger causes the action of you opening the app. The reward is what you see or experience, like that cute picture of a baby. You're then asked to make an investment, whether that's filling out your profile, responding or leaving a comment, sharing something yourself, etc. Now, it's critical to note that rewards must be variable for these habits to form otherwise the monotony would cause boredom and use would drop. If I just saw cute babies all the time, I'd get bored. I need to see links to informative articles, photos of my friends, or a funny video every once in a while to keep me guessing and keep me interested. Once this four-step process is repeated a few times, habits get formed.

As the conversation progressed, I found the second key that would unlock Susan's statement: habits take 30 days to form. A month's worth of electrons firing and dopamine spreading and all that other good brain stuff causes those synapses to build and eventually a habit is made.

MEMBERSHIP MARKETING REIMAGINED

So armed with this knowledge on how habits are formed and how long they take, I once again contemplated the sage words of Susan Greene. As I alluded to earlier, the problem of private club membership isn't the offer, it's the process. It's the way we're going about trying to sell something. If we can think of the sales process as a 30-day habit-forming process, instead of that proverbial "three-hour tour", I think success will come more easily. Those close ratios will go up. You'll turn more prospects into members. It's science.

My challenge to boards, GM / COOs, and membership directors is to begin to treat the membership sales process as a relay race spread out over 30 days. Break that down into a 4-week period where you can get a prospect immersed in your club. Give those prospects variable rewards and let them begin to associate the time spent at your club with the "good times". Get them in that habit.

In practice, this is a 40,000-foot view of how it might look. Week 1, prospects tour your facility and are introduced to key staff. Week 2, prospects are invited back to play a round of golf or hit some tennis balls or sail around your harbor so they see what it's like to decompress after a tough day at work. Week 3, invite them to have a meal at the club so they can have a sensual experience that equates your club with delight. Week 4, invite them to one of your affinity groups, like a wine club, so they can interact with folks that they can see themselves relaxing with. All the while, it's important for the membership director to follow up and make sure they are "moving the process forward," as Susan so eloquently said. After those 30 days of experiencing what it might actually be like to be a member of your club, that prospect is going to be in a much better state of mind to pull the trigger. *That's* the time to ask for the close. They'll have built those neural pathways that associate your club with pleasurable moments. They'll have made your club their habit!

This is a disruptive concept. This is outside the box. Some boards and management will be opposed to this idea. I understand that. But it takes something disruptive and scary to affect change. It's going to take a mindset shift to turn the tide and revitalize this industry we all love. This isn't the only answer, but I think it's a strong one that will help many of your clubs out there. If it's not right for yours, that's ok too. Please keep searching and remember that it's when we think we've got it all figured out that we're in the most danger.

NOTES:

_____

_____

_____

_____

_____

_____

_____

_____

_____

_____

_____

_____

_____

_____

_____

_____

_____

_____

_____

_____

_____

_____

3

CHAPTER THREE

MEMBERSHIP IS NOT A LOGICAL PURCHASE

Think about the last pair of shoes you bought. Did you buy those shoes because they had more leather per square inch than the competitor? Or did you buy them because there were exactly 48 stitches per shoe, vastly superior to the other brands? Doubtful. More likely, you bought them because they looked great on you. They looked stylish. They were comfortable. They might impress your co-workers or your friends. Heck, maybe they just filled a gap in your wardrobe for that one outfit you've been dying to wear.

We buy shoes like we buy just about everything else: for emotional reasons, not logical ones. The logical person would consider how much material we were getting for our money or the amount of steps we'd be able to take in a given pair of shoes before they wore out. But that's not why we buy them. And even if we did buy shoes for seemingly logical reasons, there would always be an emotional reason behind it. For instance, you might buy durable shoes to hike in, but the reason you hike is because you want to stay healthy, see how far you can push your body, or for the simple enjoyment of being outdoors and exploring. It's for these emotional benefits that we break out the proverbial checkbook.

Any purchase on the luxury side of the spectrum is absolutely made for emotional reasons. Cars, handbags, yachts, watches and jewelry and all those other fun things are not logical purchasing decisions. Take private club membership. It's not a very sound financial investment. You're probably not going to get any true ROI (Return on Investment) on your equity membership. Even if you did, there are many more alternative vehicles that a financial advisor would recommend. People join clubs for things like camaraderie, to achieve social status, to give their family a safe and secure environment, to experience exceptional service and for many other reasons that are not inherently logical.

When I look out into the marketplace today most clubs are portraying the wrong things. They're trying to appeal to the wrong psychological motivations. Very few are selling experiences. Most are selling a series of features instead of benefits. Just about every advertising message for a private club I see is a series of bullet point items. Bullet points are, in fact, the ultimate delivery method of logic. Think about it.

Let me know if this sounds familiar to you. It's a description of a country club I've made up, but it's one that I bet you've heard in some form another before.

"Come visit the best kept secret in Springfield. We offer a championship 18-hole Fazio designed course, 12 Har-Tru tennis courts, a modern fitness facility, an Adirondack style clubhouse and a 250-seat formal dining room."

I love Fazio designs as much as the next guy. I truly do. But will I drive 20 or more miles outside my geographical area to join a club simply because it's a Fazio design? I'm sorry, Mr. Fazio, I will not. Does that big dining room offer something different than the club down the road? Probably not. Does the style of clubhouse architecture influence my decision? Unequivocally, no. The list goes on.

All things being equal, I'm going to join the club that I feel meets my emotional needs and those of my family. Now if your club can do that better than the club down the road, that's where I'm going to apply. It's truly that simple for the vast majority of those considering joining a private club.

As such, clubs that use copywriting geared toward the emotional side of the brain would fair far better and do more to stand out from their competition. Below are a few concrete examples of how you can say the same thing, but say it in a much more effective manner by replacing logical statements with emotional ones.

Instead of This: Join us for a fun-filled open house.

Say This: You're invited to an exclusive one-day-only luxury lifestyle experience.

Instead of This: The best kept secret in South Florida.

Say This: Come explore. We've been waiting for you.

Instead of This: We offer a championship 18-hole Fazio designed course, 12 Har-Tru tennis courts, a modern fitness facility, and a 250-seat formal dining room.

Say This: Imagine the possibilities.

Understanding this concept intellectually is one thing. Putting it into practice is the hard part. I can almost guarantee you that your brain will try to fight this with every ounce of effort it can muster. Your fingers will beg you to type out that next bullet list. Something in us feels if we don't describe every last detail or squeeze in every amenity description we'll somehow miss out on that perfect member. All I can say is don't give in to that lie. Take a look at Rolex, at Chanel, at Louis Vuitton, at Mercedes and at every other brand on the luxury spectrum. They're selling an emotion. Study their ad messages and their copywriting style in their literature, on their websites and on their social media accounts. You'll find they focus on things like tradition, passion, prestige, elegance, attention to detail and the like. These are powerful motivators for those considering big-ticket items. Fight the temptation to stuff more in and edit yourself past your normal comfort level. You'll see that prospects will become much more engaged with your message.

NOTES:

_____

_____

_____

_____

_____

_____

_____

_____

_____

_____

_____

_____

_____

_____

_____

_____

_____

_____

_____

_____

_____

_____

4

CHAPTER FOUR

MEMBERSHIP IS NOT ONE SIZE FITS ALL

When was the last time you walked into a store, went up to the manager, asked what his most expensive item was and said, "I'll take that one!" How about the first time you walked into a dealership to buy a car; did you drive out of there with their top of the line model with every available option? I'd suspect that wasn't the case.

I literally cannot think of an industry that would encourage their representatives and salespeople to constantly push their top shelf offering. But that's exactly what most clubs are trying to do when they give their membership directors a directive to focus on selling the full golf membership.

About a year ago I bought my first Rolex. I didn't buy it for its flashy looks. In fact, I got one that's pretty understated. In the time I've worn it, only two or three people have even noticed. That's perfectly fine because, for me, it represented a personal achievement and a struggle that I had worked hard to overcome. I reached a goal I had set for myself and that was the reward I chose. But guess what? I didn't buy a solid gold, diamond encrusted Presidential model. Beyond looking absolutely ridiculous on *my* wrist, it was also way beyond my current budget.

Here's the crux of it though: even if I could afford a top of the line model, I don't know if I'd have the wardrobe to go along with it. I don't think I'd have enough occasions where I'd need to be dressed that formal that it would even make sense to own.

That's just me though. There are plenty of guys who could not only afford it, but it would work perfectly for the situations they find themselves in each day. That's the beauty of a diverse product line: options.

One last example—which is a favorite in our industry— booze. When you were in college, did you drink top shelf whiskey, vodka, wine, beer, etc? I didn't. Granted, I was the poor kid at the rich kid's school, American University in Washington, DC. But I was surrounded by very wealthy students. They were the sons and daughters of diplomats, tech billionaires, Saudi oil tycoons and even a former Hollywood child actor. Many could afford Louis XIII, but we mostly drank well vodka, boxed wine and Natural Light beer. That's what everyone drinks in college. It would almost be uncool not to.

Great products and great brands have options as well as systems for consumers to move through a lifecycle. They have a logical progression for folks to purchase an introductory offering and then work their way up the product line until they're comfortable making the purchase.

Apple is a shining example of how modern brands develop a product sphere that moves people up the chain. Very rarely does someone approach their brand from the top end. The iPod or iPhone is the first product most consumers will buy. As their relationship with Apple evolves, and they familiarize themselves with the features and operating systems of Apple's entry level products, they'll then begin to move onto things like an iPad, MacBook or an iMac. And only the most hardcore or professional Apple users will venture on to top-tier offerings like the Mac Pro.

When people walk into an Apple store, staff doesn't point first-time buyers toward the Mac Pros. That would almost be silly. They generally reserve that for the hardcore fanboys who have geeked out over Apple computers and products for years.

Membership brands should take a cue from one of the most savvy marketers on the planet, Tony Robbins. Tony Robbins is a motivational speaker. He has consulting clients that pay him over $100,000 per hour. That's his top-tier offering. If Tony just sold a couple of those a year, he'd be in good shape. But Tony knows he needs a product line to get people to that point. He starts off with entry-level products. These are things like books and DVDs that cost $10-25. When you're ready for the next step, you might attend one of his introductory seminars like "Unleash the Power Within." This will run folks between a few hundred dollars up to a couple grand, depending on your seat. He's got something called "Business Mastery" that will cost you upwards of $10,000. After that, only a select few inner-circle people get to pay Tony his $100k an hour.

I'm sure by now you're starting to see a formula that is used by just about every successful business out there. Start small, work your way up the product or service line.

Membership is your club's product line. Social or athletic memberships are your club's entry-level offering. A full golf membership is your club's top-of-the-line model. Why, as an industry, are we trying to do something that no other industry does? Why are we trying to put the cart before the horse?

Social members have long been the redheaded stepchildren of the private club industry. They're the ones taking up seats in the dining room. They're the ones whose kids are running around the pool. They're the ones who don't contribute a single thing to the club apart from a meager dues check each month. Isn't that right? To those who hold that opinion, I say you're absolutely wrong.

My business consultant, a kind gentleman by the name of Gary Teaney, gave me a golden nugget when I first started working with him. I really wanted to increase my sales. My goal was to double revenue. I showed him a couple ideas on how I wanted to go about prospecting. Instead he gave me a piece of advice that stuck. He told me, "Gabe, the easiest person to sell to is the one who just bought." Basically, he was telling me to focus on driving more business from my existing customers and stop putting all my focus on finding new ones. He was absolutely right. Smart businesses know that it's a much more costly proposition to prospect than to nurture the relationships you already have. Or to put it another way, it's cheaper to farm than to hunt.

When I ask membership directors if they have formed a plan to turn their social or athletic members into golf members, nearly all say no. This is dumbfounding to me. How could you not address the people who are already part of your club culture? These are the ones best suited to buy into what you're "selling". This is your low hanging fruit. They've already bought in, you just need to work them up your product line.

Five years ago a family probably joined your club that loved your brand but just didn't want or have the need for the "Presidential". Maybe it was something just like my wardrobe problem. Possibly they didn't have the time to play 4.5 hour rounds of golf, but their kids have grown and now they do. Maybe they didn't have interest in the game back then, but they're starting to feel the itch. Maybe it's just a fear of getting out on the course and looking foolish. Could a few group lessons over cocktails with the head pro make an impact? I say yes.

It's my opinion that we need to flip the script. We need to think of our membership categories as a product funnel. We need to start thinking about upgrading, instead of waiting for members to downgrade. If we don't we'll be fighting a constant uphill battle.

So there you have it. Those are three strategies—create a habit, appeal to the prospect's emotions and offer different product options—that you can implement this year in your club and start to see a major impact. I don't pretend that any of the three will be easy, and it will certainly take some time to get the buy-in of members and staff who are entrenched in their thinking and ways of doing things, but I firmly believe if these changes are made it will pay dividends to you and your club.

NOTES:

_____
_____
_____
_____
_____
_____
_____
_____
_____
_____
_____
_____
_____
_____
_____
_____
_____
_____
_____
_____

5

CHAPTER FIVE

THE ESSENTIAL TOOLS OF CLUB MARKETING

Okay, so now you know what to do once you have that prospect in hand—but how do you drive them to your club in the first place? The following is a set of marketing tools and best practices for membership directors and those sitting on membership committees. I've tried to make this list as comprehensive as possible. While new mediums and marketing channels may come into fashion, the foundational concepts and techniques described here will always remain constant and applicable. I hope this becomes a handy reference guide that you refer back to often in your club membership marketing strategies.

THE IMPORTANCE OF DATA & SURVEYING

At the last membership and marketing conference I attended, Rick Coyne founder of ClubMark and an industry legend, began his keynote presentation by asking a series of questions to the audience. First he asked them, "How many of you know the average income of your membership?" Amidst the crowd of over 300 membership professionals, barely a handful answered yes. The next question he asked was, "How many of you know the average drive time to your club?" Even fewer hands went up this time. He then asked, "How many of you know the average age of your membership?" This time about a quarter of the room raised their hands. To this response he told them, "It's good to see that at least you know that, but unfortunately that doesn't matter. You need to be thinking about the age of the members that will make up your clubs in five years or ten years." He was right. This simple exercise shined the light on a problem that is pervasive in the private club industry: there is a lack of data both being captured and analyzed usefully.

There isn't a successful marketer out there, in any industry, who doesn't have a firm grasp of their target market with a psychographic and demographic profile. Marketing success and quantifiable data go hand in hand. In the words of Ray Cronin, co-founder of Club Benchmarking, "Without facts you're only left opinion."

As someone tasked with the membership and marketing responsibilities of your club, it's essential that you first start with a factual foundation of your market. I would highly recommend you conduct surveys of both your membership and the local community.

For the majority of clubs, their members will come from a relatively immediate vicinity. I would suggest a 10-mile radius as a good starting point. This usually covers about a 15-minute or less drive time, which is an ideal trip for most folks who frequent their club.

Within that 10-mile radius, you'll want to pull some demographic data. I would recommend you at least find out the median age, home value and household income. You can also lay some psychographic profiling on top of that, which is a fancy word that marketers use for interests and hobbies. Golf interest, tennis interest and water sports interest would be helpful, depending on the amenities that your club offers. Also things like an interest in "fine dining" or "wine enthusiast" may be something you can use to your advantage. Going even deeper on the programming side, if you're a family-oriented club or have activities geared toward adolescents and teens, you may want to look for the presence of children. There is data like this available from many vendors.

Here's an insider tip: oftentimes, list agents or brokers will give you these basic numbers called "count requests" without having to purchase a list. If you can get a zip code breakdown, you'll know what areas you should target with your marketing, whether it's digital or in print. This free data is invaluable in helping you understand your local community and your market potential.

Without accurate data, you're flying blind and making assumptions. That's the worst thing you can do as a marketer. It's sent many clubs and businesses under. I don't want that to happen to you, so make sure you never skip this step.

Surveying is another essential way to understand your prospective market. Specialty firms like ClubMark out of Dallas, Texas help their clients gather valuable information that can go a long way to determining the viability of a certain marketing program or amenity offering. For instance a survey of 10,000 residents in your local market might yield insights like it's time to build that swimming pool, or there's a real need for a great fine dining experience in the community. These insights are priceless. It's a snapshot of your audience in real time. It's like fishing with a bazooka, as opposed to a BB gun. You'll catch a lot more prospects if you have more information.

WHY MOST CAMPAIGNS FAIL

The vast majority of marketing campaigns, whether in the club business or outside, are complete and utter failures. After a couple of duds people get gun-shy. They question whether that particular marketing method works anymore. They usually end up walking away from the current approach and scrapping the idea of marketing altogether or they try something else new in hopes that it will be the panacea they've been looking for.

In reality, the problem probably wasn't the medium they chose at all. It's that they didn't use that marketing channel in an effective manner or they didn't do the research on how to reach the right market with the right message. Marketing failures are most often the result of poor planning, poor goal setting, poor data tracking and poor follow up. For a campaign to be successful, you need to execute on each of these things. In the following sections, I'm going to show you how to do it most effectively.

PLANNING & GOAL SETTING

Too often, the process of creating goals and ways to track them is an afterthought. It's often left until after the ads have been designed and the ad space has been purchased or the campaign has been initiated.

Worse yet, I see far too many marketing managers whose only goal is to break even or better. If you've ever uttered the words, "I just want to make back more than I spend," you have been in that camp. That is a defeatist attitude, and often the first step to advertising failure.

I'm a firm believer in the law of attraction, having seen it proved true over and over again in my business and personal life. So when I hear those types of statements uttered, I cringe inside. Full disclosure, when I first started in business I uttered those same words, too. Guess what? I got what I put out there, or worse, every time.

Then there are the ones who have no goal in place whatsoever. They just want more members, period. What's really scary is this is not the minority. The vast majority of clients that come through the doors of my agency are in this camp. They just want something designed for some random ad space they purchased because it was affordable and the salesperson caught them at the right time.

Here's my promise to you: If you don't know what a win looks like, you will always lose. So I implore you to start tracking everything you do when it comes to your advertising. At the very least you should be tracking the amount of leads you receive directly from your campaign, how many of those leads convert and become customers (conversions) and what ROI is.

Keep in mind that your ROI should be calculated in terms of Lifetime Customer Value (LCV). The LCV is what one person, whether member or guest, spends with you, minus your costs, over the course of their relationship with your club.

As you run new campaigns, be sure to compare them against the results of prior campaigns. Look for any anomalies and notate them. You might notice a big spike or a big drop against previous data that signals something is working or not.

SPLIT TESTING AND FOCUS GROUPS

There's no such thing as a sure thing, but wouldn't it be nice to have some inside information that would help you begin the process on an optimistic note? That's where split testing and focus groups come in! These easy-to-implement mini studies help you get an early grasp on what will work and what won't. I always recommend that my clients use them, and they're easier and less expensive than you think to put into action. In fact, I have a little hack I like to use which I'll tell you about at the end of this section.

Split testing, also known as A/B testing, is simply trying out two versions of an ad on a small scale and seeing which performs better. Ad "A" might have a slightly different headline than ad "B". Ad "B" might have a different color button than ad "A". Once you determine which version results in more leads or sales, you can scale it up and start to spend more of your marketing dollars with it.

The split testing method works great for web landing pages, eblasts, web ads and direct mail campaigns. It's harder to test for a billboard, magazine ads and other traditional media like television and radio ads without increasing your advertising budget significantly. That is, unless you know my hack. More on that shortly.

So when you're going to spend a significant amount of your budget in ad placement, and you only have one shot to do it right, I'd highly recommend using a focus group. A focus group is smaller set of individuals that are your core target demographic for your product or service. You might show them your proposed ad and see what their reaction is. You might even give them a couple of options to choose from and see what resonates with them.

In general, I recommend you have a short multiple-choice questionnaire that they fill out. And, if you do employ multiple choice questions, be sure to include space for them to write in their own thoughts and observations beyond your line of questioning. You never know what gems might come out of it. In case you want some extra help with your focus group questionnaire, I've got a short sample questionnaire that you can use as a starting point. Visit aluisy.com/questionnaire to download it.

If you noticed above, I was very specific that a focus group should be made up of your core demographic. I want to really drive this distinction home. I see many entrepreneurs asking their Facebook friends for advice on their ads and that's really a bad idea for a couple of reasons. Firstly, the responses they get back are rarely objective. Your friends and family have a deeper desire to please you or be a cheerleader for you than the public at large.

As such, you're more likely to get skewed results that are higher in praise and lower in critical advice that will help you execute your campaign with better results. Secondly, the opinion of folks outside of your core demographic just doesn't matter. They're not your ideal customers, or in this case potential members.

The only, and I mean *only*, opinion that matters is someone who is most likely going to become a member. An art director's opinion, a designer's opinion, a marketing person's opinion, a partner's opinion, an employee's opinion and anyone else's should all be taken under advisement, but should never be taken as gospel. There is always a right and wrong choice when it comes to design. The right design choice is the one that your target demographic will respond to. It's the one that sells. Focus groups can help you make the right design choice. Art is subjective, design doesn't have to be.

A/B TESTING ON A BUDGET HACK

Most clubs are essentially small business. As such there's a good chance you don't have the budget to have a dud. You might be spending a few weeks or even a few months' profit on an ad campaign and you need it to work the first time around. You may not have the budget to split test ideas and you may not have the funds to run a focus group. Luckily, I've got a great hack for you.

My trick is to use Facebook advertising, which is a very cost-effective way to reach a large audience. You can test your ad there for pennies per person. Using the Facebook ad manager, you can choose a specific demographic that would fall within your target membership area. You can get really specific into behaviors and interests as well. Facebook also makes it a snap to split test. Set a budget of something like $20 and see what ad gets the most engagement in the form of likes and / or clicks. When you have a decisive champ, you can then invest your marketing dollars into that billboard, full-page spread or other expensive ad placement, much more confident that you've got a winner!

As I said earlier, be sure to compare the results of new campaigns against the results of prior campaigns. If there are anomalies, spikes, or drops, make a note and then analyze the reason behind them. It's usually a sign of how well a strategy is working.

CREATING A FOLLOW-UP PLAN

Another reason most marketing campaigns fail is because there was no roadmap created for following up with leads and prospects. To be honest, early on in my business career, I made this mistake many times myself. It's easy to do. You get caught up in how great your offer is or how impactful the design looks and you assume that people will be banging down your door to get in. Even Apple, when they launch a new iPhone, despite all of their fanboys lining up days before to get one, makes sure to develop a complete email follow-up campaign each time a new product launches. If it works for them, there's no reason we shouldn't all be doing it.

I found an interesting statistic that I want to share with you. It has been attributed to the National Sales Executive

Association. They broke down the sales follow-up process in the following way:

48% of salespeople never follow up with a prospect

25% of salespeople make a second contact and stop

12% of salespeople only make three contacts and stop

Only 10% of salespeople make more than 3 contacts

2% of sales are made on the first contact

3% of sales are made on the second contact

5% of sales are made on the third contact

10% of sales are made on the fourth contact

80% of sales are made on the fifth to twelfth contact

Eighty percent—a vast majority—of sales are made after multiple contacts. That's a number you need to pay attention to. It dramatically puts things into perspective and I hope it lights a fire in you to take a hard look at your own follow-up process.

So how does one actually improve their follow-up strategy? For me, it begins and ends with having a good customer relationship management system (CRM). Good CRMs will be able to track the stages of the deal cycle, remind you when it's time to follow up with a prospect, and give you detailed reporting on what's working effectively and what is not. I consider my CRM to be my electronic accountability partner. It's something to hold me to what I said I would do and to keep me focused on moving the sale forward.

I'm by no means a CRM expert, but I am a user and self-proclaimed computer geek so people ask me what they should look for when they are going to buy one. My primary advice is to find a company that has great, and I mean *really great*, customer service. You will inevitably need help figuring something out and if it takes three days to get a response back from the support team you've cost yourself and your club valuable time and expense, not to mention the lost opportunity cost.

My second criterion is that it be intuitive. If you can't poke around and pretty much figure it out, it's probably too complicated and not worth the hassle of learning. All great software should aid you in your processes, not get in your way. What's the point of owning a Ferrari if you can't figure out how to drive a stick shift?

Lastly, it should have some particular features that will save you so much time it is a joy, not a chore to open up and use. The ones that are important for me are:

- The ability to automate tasks such as sending emails to prospects

- The ability to quickly see where prospects are in the various stages of my pipeline

- The ability to email directly from the CRM rather having to open up a separate program

- The ability to quickly generate basic reports like close ratios

- The ability to create tasks and get reminders to follow up

- The ability to track whether or not someone opens an email or clicks a link

One of the most invaluable tools that a good CRM will have is the ability to set up an autoresponder campaign. This is a series of emails to a prospects and it eliminates the excuse of forgetting to follow up. Auto responders have become very advanced these days. They can be triggered automatically by someone signing up for your mailing list or downloading a brochure on your website (a tactic I highly recommend for private clubs). They can then send particular emails based on the behavior of the prospect.

For instance, if the prospect clicks on a particular link in email one, they will be served a second email that is different than if they had not clicked. If you build your system right you can literally put your email on autopilot. That will free you up to do more important tasks. So many people, including myself, get bogged down with email. This will help you be much more productive.

KEY PERFORMANCE INDICATORS

The private club industry historically has been a poor steward of data gathering and analysis. I'm not sure why, maybe it's due to the unique structure of customers who are also the owners, but it seems our industry lags behind most others by five to ten years in many ways. One way it has lagged behind, and done so to its detriment, is in the area of tracking and benchmarking. Luckily there are some good managers, directors and vendors who are turning the tide.

For me there are a 22 must-know statistics for anyone tasked with membership. If you're serving as a membership director or if you're sitting on the membership committee, you need to know these 22 KPIs frontwards and backwards. These numbers allow you to properly set and track goals, target the right membership prospects, cut the best deals with vendors and ad agencies, and communicate with your board and members. The problem is there are very few people out there who know them, let alone keep track of them. This is the stuff they never prepared you for in college, they don't talk about at conferences, and you don't have time to figure out on your own. But these are the critical elements to successful membership marketing:

1. Average age of your membership

2. Average drive time to your club

3. Average age within that drive time

4. Average income of your membership

5. Average income within the drive time

6. What One Member is Worth

7. CPM

8. Reach

9. Cost Per impression

10. Cost Per Click

11. Conversion Rate

12. Cost Per Conversion

13. Member Usage Rate

14. Retention rate

15. Average Membership Lifespan

16. Average Age of Retirement

17. Referral rate

18. Open rate

19. CTR

20. Close ratio

21. Average Time to Close (TTC)

22. Return on Investment

If you can get a firm grasp of each of these numbers in relation to your club marketing, you will become what I like to call "board bulletproof." Knowing these 22 statistics will prepare you for any question that could ever arise in the boardroom or in management meetings. Now that you know what they are, let's break them down one by one.

KPI #1 - AVERAGE AGE OF YOUR MEMBERSHIP

The average age of your membership is a baseline statistic that is important in determining the overall health of your club. It's also a number that prospective members are often going to want to know to see how well they'll fit in. Today's healthy clubs often have a good mixture of age ranges at the club.

Clubs whose average age is in the 70s or in the mid to late 60s should be worried. If that's you, it's of vital importance to work on lowering that number as it is not sustainable. It's nearly impossible to attract millennials or even Generation X-ers to a club like this. That means, in as short as five or as long as ten years, if nothing changes, you're going to need 100% turnover in order to buy yourself another five or ten. At that point, you're a glorified senior care facility.

If you want to lower that average age, the best way to attack it is to start from the top. Don't try to go after 40 year olds, start with high 50s and slowly work your way down. Try to gradually lower that number five years at a time.

Some steps that you could consider to lower your average age include creating a legacy membership for the children of your senior members to encourage getting some fresh blood into the club. Try adding membership categories such as a young executive membership to your offerings. Most of all, I would suggest taking a hard look at your programming and amenities. Build a gym if you don't have one. Expand it if you do. Don't add a pickleball court as that's a game for seniors. Instead, add something young families would enjoy, like a splash pad for the kids. Begin to host a mixture of events that cater to different age groups. These are just a few ideas; you'll have to see what works for your club. As a membership director or a committee chair, this should be your sole focus until it's solved.

KPI #2 - AVERAGE DRIVE TIME

It's important to know where your members are coming from. Average drive time takes away the guesswork. There's a direct correlation between the time spent in the car and the likelihood of someone joining, or keeping their club membership. As much as clubs would like to tout their famous course architect, the fact of the matter is, proximity is a more important factor. This becomes more apparent each year as our culture develops an on-demand mentality.

The data shows that most clubs get their members within a 15-minute drive time of their property. It makes perfect sense. Drives longer than that begin to noticeably cut into the valuable leisure time clubs provide.

If you can go even a little deeper with your survey data, you'll know the three or four key zip codes your members are coming from. Those are the ones to target more of your time and energy on with your marketing campaigns. People often think direct mail is a costly and unproductive marketing channel, but when you're laser focused on a particular area that has a high concentration of the type of people that make up your club, you're going to set yourself up for more success.

KPI #3 - AVERAGE AGE WITHIN THAT DRIVE TIME

Average age within the drive time of your members to your club sounds like a combination of the two previous KPIs, but this is something different altogether. Simply put, this KPI is a gauge of your club's local community demographics. Basically, a healthy club should be in line with the community at large. If your club has an average age of 65, but your community has an average of 52, it's time to take a second look at why. This is a simple thing, but so many overlook it.

KPI #4 - AVERAGE INCOME

This basic stat is another that most membership professionals I've met don't have a firm grasp on. Sometimes I'll ask them, "Just take a guess or give me a ballpark." Often, the response is a shoulder shrug. I'm kind of used to it now, but the first few times it happened I almost fell out of my seat. Without this number it's nearly impossible to buy advertising effectively. Having this number allows you to pick and choose publications, targeted mail lists, target social media profiles and just about every form of mass media properly.

Most traditional media outlets will give you a breakdown of their reach. They usually refer to this as a media kit. Inside, they'll tell you the average age, income, the mixture of gender and other facts. It's important that you look at these statistics and make sure that their audience matches your target demographic. That's why you need to know this number.

KPI #5 - AVERAGE INCOME WITHIN YOUR CLUB'S DRIVE TIME

Similar to #3 above, it's important to know what kind of income folks have in your local community within the range you've determined is drivable. This information will give you an accurate depiction of how easy or difficult it is to find members who can afford your initiation fee and dues. It will also give you a clearer picture of where your potential members can come from. It's important to pinpoint the right neighborhoods and zip codes where there's correlation.

This number may influence your decision making process when it comes to raising or lowering your dues structure. You might find there are big pockets of wealth which would signal an increase is sustainable. You might find the inverse is true, and consider opening up some new membership categories.

KPI #6 - WHAT ONE MEMBER IS WORTH (LMV)

This is a number that a good general manager would be able to tell you off the top of his or her head. However, I find it's not well understood or tracked by membership directors and often not taken into consideration by membership committees. I think knowing this number might just be the most crucial KPI of all, because it should serve as the basis for setting your marketing budget.

It's not uncommon that I come across a struggling club and during our discovery session I'll ask the simple question, "So what's an average member worth to you?" The response that comes out first is rarely the number we reach at the end of the discussion. Usually I'll get an answer that calculates the initiation fee and the monthly dues, possibly over the course of one year.

At this point I'll ask, in the case of a golf club, if the members occasionally take their meals at the club. Of course the answer is, "Yes." Then I'll go on to ask if they ever attend any of the clubs events and parties? Do they ever rent the events space for a party, wedding, or meeting? Do they bring guests and pay cart fees or tennis court fees? Do they ever purchase anything from the pro shop? Yes, yes, yes and yes.

Now we're getting somewhere. So now we've found that one member is worth a whole lot more than their dues. Then I ask a question that even the sharpest of owners, GMs, and membership directors rarely account for. Do they ever refer their friends? At this point I've really got them thinking.

You see, until you have the numbers right on what a member is actually worth, there's no point in trying to figure out how much you should spend on marketing to them. There's also no way to accurately gauge their impact on your bottom line, or to what means you should go to retain them. That's why I think this just might be the most vital number to keep track of them all.

Once we know what this number is, we can subtract it by the average expenses per member over the course of a year and multiply it by the average number of years a member stays at the club. This will help us determine what I like to call the Lifetime Membership Value or LMV for short. The LMV is the main number that should be used when budgeting your marketing efforts. If you know the LMV of a member at your club is $100,000, you could take a percentage of that to determine what should go into your marketing budget. I tell my clients that 8% is a good number to shoot for. This is a number commonly used by businesses in varying industries.

So if your goal is to add 10 new members in a season you would take 8% of $100,000 which is $8,000 and multiply that by 10. This would give you a marketing budget of $80,000. That would be a pretty reasonable number to work with by most estimations. Hopefully you now understand how useful this number can be.

KPI #7 - CPM

CPM is a term you will often run across when placing advertising. It's a commonly used number in both digital and traditional media. CPM stands for cost per mille. In layman's terms, it's the cost you will pay to reach every 1,000 people.

So if you are buying a 5,000-person mailing list and the CPM is $100, you will pay $500 for that list. Dividing that number by 1,000 will give you the cost to reach one person. So in our example of the $100 CPM, it will cost us 10 cents to reach each person. That's a pretty good CPM no matter what the medium.

KPI #8 - REACH

Reach is a term that is commonly used on social media advertising like Facebook or Instagram. Reach is how many people were served a particular message. Reach grows exponentially when people share content across their own networks of friends and family.

You'll want to keep track of the reach that certain posts or digital ads have. This will give you a good idea of what types of things are working and not. If one of your posts blows up, compare it to other recent posts and try to figure out why. Was it because you used an image of a person? Was it because it was a catchy quote? Was it due to the time of day you posted it? All this can make a difference. It's your job to figure out what worked and why.

KPI #9 - COST PER IMPRESSION

Cost per impression is a term used in both digital and print marketing. Unfortunately, the word impression isn't used like the dictionary definition. An impression in digital marketing terms occurs every time your ad appears on a web page whether it's seen or not by the viewer. An impression in a print publication is a combination of the print run and the number of times that publication is typically shared. It doesn't mean anyone saw the ad, just that they had the opportunity to do so. So you're definitely not guaranteed to make an "impression" on them. If your ad is on the page, even way down at the bottom, you're paying for it.

Cost per impression, or CPI for short, coupled with CPL and CPC, which we'll explore next, is a good way to determine the effectiveness of your ad messages.

KPI #10 - COST PER CLICK

Cost Per Click, or CPC, tracks how many of those impressions take the next action online, and that means clicks to your web page. This is one of the most important stats you'll need to keep track of when it comes to digital marketing. This number will give you an indication of how effective your ad or your post is.

You'll want to keep the cost side of this number as low as possible. As of this book's writing, for Google Adwords that means under $2 in most cases. With Facebook ads you should be able to stay under $1 for most audiences. This number does vary depending on many factors. Pay per click ads online use a bidding system. The more people who are bidding for the same audience or the same keywords, the more it will drive this price up. In the private club industry, there won't be much competition though, so you should be able to keep this number within something reasonable. Slip and fall attorneys won't have it so lucky. I've seen CPC's of $15 or more because there are far more personal injury attorneys in the world, vying for your attention, and that makes the advertising that much more competitive!

KPI #11 - CONVERSION RATE

The Conversion Rate is a percentage of people who became actual leads or prospects from your ad. With digital marketing, you can find the conversion rate by taking the number of people who filled out your form, called, or contacted you in some way and dividing that by the number of people who clicked on the ad or opened the email. This number basically judges the effectiveness of your landing page or website.

I like to use this statistic in traditional campaigns as well. Here's an example: If a magazine has a distribution of 100,000 readers and you get 100 calls from your ad, you have a conversion rate of .01%.

KPI #12 - COST PER CONVERSION

Cost Per Conversion is a crucially important statistic to make sure that the ads you're placing online are actually turning into prospects for your club. This is really the ultimate litmus test that your offer and your targeting are working as you planned. If I could only keep track of one stat with my online ads, this would be it, because it's the one that truly matters.

You can have great reach and great CPC, but if you don't convert any of them –get them to fill out your form, send you an email, pick up the phone, or walk in the door— you've really just got some pretty stats. It would be like a basketball team getting hundreds of rebounds and steals, but not scoring any points. It looks great in the box score, but it's only the win that counts on their record.

KPI #13 - MEMBER USAGE RATES

Even though member usage rates are gathered after joining, I think they are an important stat to track for marketing professionals, management and committee members. Why? Because it costs the club far less to retain a member than to market to and find new ones.

At a minimum, I would begin tracking how often members access certain areas of the club such as the golf course, gym or fitness facility, tennis courts, pool area, restaurants, bars and other specialty spaces your club might have.

Of course, you can track with paper sheets and boots on the ground but, with geo-fencing capabilities that are now standard on a number of apps in our industry, tracking this type of data is less invasive and cumbersome. Members can have an app installed on their phones and mobile devices that register each time they visit a certain area of the club. Beacons, which are small devices, can be placed in strategic spots around the club and be set to certain radiuses. As an example, you might put one at the front desk of your fitness facility and have it set to a 10-yard radius. When a member with the app installed passes by, it will pick the signal up via Wi-Fi or Bluetooth and log that activity in a software program.

Advanced CRM systems from many of the leading industry vendors like Clubessential will store the data and help you build a profile for each member. A good system can let you set thresholds for when you want to be notified of member activity or lack thereof. For instance, if a member is only using the club once every couple of months, that's a signal that you should reach out to them and find out why. It might be that they are on vacation, but it just might be that they don't realize the great new events you have planned. This type of outreach based on empirical data just might save you a member and your job!

KPI #14 - RETENTION RATE

Retention rates determine both how well you've done your job and how much harder you'll have to work in the next period. This number is shown as a percentage. Here's how it works: if you had 500 members at the start of the season and 485 were left at the end of the season, your retention rate would be 97%. Note: This number should not indicate new members that were gained during the season. That would throw the statistic off.

If your retention rate stays high after an increase in membership, it probably means you added members to your club that were the right cultural and social fit. If it begins to lower even after the addition of new members, you might want to take a look at why. For instance, I've seen clubs lower their initiation fees and see retention rates plummet because the folks that became members later realized they really couldn't afford the club. Since their investment was low, it didn't hurt so much to leave.

Retention rates give you a solid baseline for your goal setting. By knowing this number, you'll be better able to come up with a net membership increase goal. You'll already be able to estimate how many members will leave in the coming season, and add that to your new membership goal.

KPI #15- AVERAGE MEMBERSHIP LIFESPAN

The average membership lifespan is exactly what it sounds like. It's the average number of years members stay at your club. This is another statistic that will help with goal setting. It will give you an idea of turnover and help you determine how many memberships need to be filled to account for the loss.

Also important, it should help you determine the Lifetime Membership Value or LMV which is crucial to budgeting as I explained previously.

Here's a membership retention hack. If you know that your average member stays for 5 years, I'd suggest you take a look at those members in the 3 to 7 year range and reach out to them. Invite them to lunch or send them a personal note to see how they are doing and what else they might be wanting from the club. Like we said before, keeping members happy and retained should be just as important as finding new ones.

KPI #16- AVERAGE AGE OF RETIREMENT

This is a big cliff you need to see coming. If your average age of retirement from the club is 72 and your average age of membership is 67 or within 5 years of that range, your club is going to be in trouble. I know some clubs in this situation and it's not pretty. Just make sure you are working to get your club at least 10 years below this threshold.

KPI #17- REFERRAL RATE

This metric tracks how many new members are coming directly from member referrals.

If you don't know this, how do you know if your membership is sustainable? There are a number of insights that can be gleaned from this number. One being the satisfaction of the membership at large. It's not a secret that members who are happy with the facilities, programming and service will tell their friends. When those things go south they won't, and they'll eventually resign.

This number will also help you determine how much time, effort and money should go into an internal campaign vs. an external campaign. When referral rates are low, it might signal it's time to roll out a structured membership referral program. Those programs work well if there's some gamified element. By that I mean, maybe the top referrer wins an exclusive trip, or gets some sort of preferred status. Heck, even a better parking spot is all the motivation some people need. Remember, humans are wired for competition, so do something that gets their competitive juices flowing whenever possible.

Results can be tracked and displayed in a central location like an announcement board.

Another thing you'll want to look deeper at within this category is who your top referrers are. These folks are probably natural connectors and most likely have a deep network. The connector personality is one of the driving forces in sweeping change. These individuals can almost single-handedly put your club on the map. Find out who they are and invite these folks into your office for a meeting. You just might be surprised what comes from it.

KPI #18- OPEN RATE

This is a number that is tracked specifically in email campaigns. It's simply a percentage of how many people opened your email when it was in their inbox vs. trashing it immediately. Open rates can be affected by a number of factors, including time of day the email was sent, how compelling your subject line was and how good your list is.

There are some benchmarks you should be aware of. With a cold list, usually a purchased list of non-members, you can expect to get lower open rates. 18% and below is what I would consider low. 10% and lower would be dreadful. Anywhere from 18%-35% would be good. With a warm list of members and prospects, I think 35-50% is a good average or a goal to set. For hot lists, something you target at specific members such as a golf events update that is sent to only the golfers at your club, you can get some really good results. Look to be in the 75% range or thereabouts.

If your emails are falling outside these rough benchmarks, you may want to first test a new subject line. You just might not have grabbed their attention. Good subject lines are usually seven words or less. I've found that seven is the magic number with attention spans being so low these days.

The subject line should create an urge to open and offer only a taste of what's inside. It should scream, "open me!" Think of it as the first call to action. Don't think you need to explain everything, just whet their appetite. Get them to want to open that email. If your offer is a free preview round of golf, then don't write "Redeem Your Free Preview Round of Golf." You've already given everything away up front. Instead try, "An Exclusive VIP Offer Inside." In this scenario, you've asked them to open the email and a taste of what they will find. You can hit them with the details and explain more within the email itself. All you want to do with the subject line is tease it.

Because email tracking is very accurate, you can resend your email to those who didn't open it the first time with a new subject line. A good email system or CRM will be able to let you narrow down your list to those who did not open the previous eblast and let you send to them only. This often works wonders because maybe the day they received it they were extremely busy or possibly the subject line just didn't speak to them. When you tweak and resend, you'll find many folks will open it on the second attempt. I'd recommend waiting a few days after the first email was sent to do this but no longer than a week. We'll discuss more about email later in the book.

KPI #19 - CLICK THRU RATE (CTR)

Click Thru Rate is a percentage of people who clicked a link. This statistic is used both in email campaigns and pay per click ads online. This number judges the effectiveness of your copy and call to action. If it's strong you're going to see this number get bigger and that's what you want. For emails, a CTR of 5% or higher is a good benchmark. For things like online pay per click ads on Google or Facebook, look to be in the 2% or higher range.

KPI #20 - CLOSE RATIO

Close ratio is a measure of how effective you are as a salesperson combined with how strong your offer and brand recognition is. First off, there is no such thing as a 100% close ratio. Rejection is a part of any salesperson's job. And to be honest, you wouldn't be doing your job if you sold everyone. It's just as important for someone to be the right fit for the club as it is to reach your membership goal. Adding the wrong members to the club is a two-fold problem. Firstly, they'll inevitably resign. Secondly, you're existing members and staff may be affected. It's a one rotten apple spoils the bunch scenario. It's best to weed out some folks in the beginning.

I don't have a benchmark of where you should be for this statistic. This really depends on a lot of factors. But what I will tell you is that you should continually work to improve this number. It's also a way to let you know how active you need to be. If it takes ten prospects touring your club to garner one new member and you have a goal of 5 new members in a month, you better make sure you get at least 50 people through your door.

KPI #21 - AVERAGE TIME TO CLOSE (TTC)

This is a stat few keep track of, but it's quite helpful in planning a campaign and keeping yourself on track. Your average time to close is the average time it takes for a prospect to first be introduced to your brand or marketed to until they apply. It's going to be different for every club. Earlier in this book, in the Membership is Not a Sprint section, I outlined a plan for a one month TTC. You may find your time to close is a week, a month or even as long as a year. It doesn't matter what it is, as long as you plan for it. Don't set unattainable goals like closing 10 new memberships in 30 days if you're average TTC is 60 days and you have no prospects.

KPI #22 RETURN ON INVESTMENT - ROI

Before you skip this section because you know it, let me warn you that you might be missing out on some things. Most calculate their return on investment by simply subtracting what the campaign cost them to design and insert from the revenue that resulted. They forget their own time spent which is often valuable time. At a minimum, there's a healthy salary or an hourly rate to account for. In the cases where committees met to discuss and strategize, this number is compounded.

Lastly, there is the lost opportunity cost. When you put energy and resources into something that underperforms it takes away from other activities you could've been doing. This is where a dud can get extremely expensive from an ROI perspective. Make sure you take everything into account when determining an ROI.

BONUS KPI - PASS THRU RATE

Pass thru rate is a statistic that magazine and newspaper publishers don't want you to know about or understand. It's their dirty little secret, but I'm going to let you in on it. Often publishers will tout their huge readership numbers (or reach). It will make their CPM look incredibly inexpensive. Imagine reaching 300,000 readers for just a $1,000 ad! Sounds too good to be true, right? It is.

You have to watch out for pass thru. Pass thru is what the publisher *estimates* will happen. Their distribution might be only 50,000, but they assume people will share their issue with 6 of their friends and family after they read it. That's how they inflate their numbers. Unless it's a Playboy magazine and a group of middle school boys, I'm here to tell you it's not happening. Make sure you ask the sales rep for the actual distribution numbers. Furthermore, make sure they're not just dropping them off at restaurants in bundles of 50 to never be picked up or see the light of day. That's another way they pad their stats.

CONCLUSION

Now that you're armed with these metrics and how they work, you're going to be fully prepared to answer any questions that come up in the boardroom related to the strength and weakness of your campaigns. You'll take the guesswork out of the membership marketing process, and you'll be able to correctly forecast your membership numbers.

NOTES:

6

CHAPTER SIX

MARKETING TACTICS & STRATEGY

I n this chapter we're going to take a deeper dive into the process of marketing your club's membership. We're going to cover both traditional and digital marketing strategies as well as public relations. I'm even going to give you some advice on emerging trends and what you should be paying attention to and the ones you should skip out on.

I want you to see all your options, because when you're putting together a marketing strategy or campaign it's important to diversify. Don't let yourself get caught in the trap of tunnel vision or thinking that doing one thing is going to get you and your club the result you want. I run into many membership directors who just decide to do things on a whim or a flavor of the month. Don't let that be you. You should know what marketing mediums are at your disposal and which you plan to use strategically *before* you spend that first marketing dollar.

Also I want you to be aware of what's coming next that's important versus what's simply a trend and fad. Something new and shiny is going to pop up every year. While being an early adopter is often rewarded for marketing channels that actually "make it", most new marketing fads fail soon after they get hot. Why is that? Mostly it's because people don't want to be marketed to. Every year a new social networking site pops up and the marketers rush to try it and capture a fresh, new audience. Then users leave because they wanted to discover something cool, not be sold to.

In marketing, past results are a poor predictor of future success. Just because a certain marketing channel worked for you last season doesn't mean it will this year. While you should have a good grasp of what you think will work based on past results you should never throw all your eggs into one basket. I've seen too many clubs and businesses fail when they took that approach because they "knew" it was going to be a sure thing.

You should also be willing to try new things out. Take at least 10% of your budget and try something new this year. You might hit a jackpot. Worst case, you'll learn a lesson that will serve you down the road. For example, I learned what worked with live streaming when I started using the site Blab.im. I figured out how to capture an audience, how to entertain and how to effectively use video to build awareness and buzz. After a year, Blab shut down, but the lessons I learned on how it worked translated to Facebook Live which has become an even more powerful force. The techniques I honed in one area helped me shorten the learning curve on the other. As long as you're finding out what works and what doesn't, there's no such thing as a marketing failure.

ANALOG / TRADITIONAL MARKETING STRATEGIES

In this section we will cover the strategies most would consider traditional. Most traditional strategies rely heavily on printed materials and direct communication. These strategies are time tested and are still valid. In some cases, traditional marketing strategies can be extraordinarily effective precisely for the fact that many people have given up on them in favor of digital strategies.

Take direct mail for instance. I've had some campaigns that absolutely crushed it, garnering as many as 20 members in one mailing, with a return on investment of over 2,000%! How is it possible? I chalk it up to the fact that many have abandoned it, creating a self-fulfilling prophecy that print is dead. I think it's very much alive. In the world of marketing, just like anything else, one man's trash is another man's treasure.

MEMBER REFERRALS

Historically this was the only form of marketing a club could do. Today it's just as important as ever. A big part of your job as a membership director or committee member should be to ask your members to spread the word. However, getting them to spread the word is easier said than done.

Today people are busier and more distracted than they've ever been before. For that reason, it's important that you give your members the right tools and make it easy for them to refer their friends and colleagues. It's also important to remind them from time to time. This section is going to focus on just that.

WHY MEMBERS REFER

There's one simple reason that one to one referrals work—we humans want to connect and share our *good* experiences. Good is an important distinction here. If you're a social media user, especially on Facebook or LinkedIn, you've probably noticed the majority of posts people make about their daily lives are positive. Sure, they might harangue a politician or some other world issue, but when they talk about themselves and what they are up to, by and large it's in a positive light. In fact, one might be led to believe that the majority of their friends live perfect lives full of excitement, passion and adventure. Of course, in reality, this is not the case. People are burdened by bills, kids get sick, cars break down and a lot of crap happens. Most people only show us a fraction of their life and leave out all those ugly bits.

People also share their once-in-a-lifetime experiences or things they find extraordinary. They rarely post about their day-to-day activities or the mundane routines they've got themselves stuck in. Once again, it's that 5% of their life that they let other people see.

When your club becomes that 5% for people, they'll let the world know, quite literally. This communication isn't limited to social media either, it happens via phone calls, emails, conversations and every other way humans connect. This means you have to provide exceptional life-changing moments that delight the body and the mind.

You also have to surprise and surpass their expectations as well as create experiences out of the ordinary moments. That's the key ingredient to getting members to refer. It sounds relatively simple, but it's extremely difficult to do.

My challenge to you is to find what can you do this month, this week, or better yet today that will surprise and delight someone at your club? What exceptional moment can you create? How can you break someone's routine in a positive way? Figure this out and you'll start creating what I like to call, brand champions. These are your "fanboys" and "fangirls" that will rave about you. What's great about a private club is, because of their ownership stake, they'll be raving about themselves, too. We all know people like to do that!

WHEN TO ASK FOR THE REFERRAL

My own business consultant told me early on, "The easiest person to sell is the one who just bought." Those words have proven true time and time again in my business. Why does this statement ring true in every industry? Because when someone has just purchased something, they are emotionally engaged and they are excited. They've also made a decision that they want to believe with all of their heart and soul was the right one. It's something of a self-fulfilling prophecy in the buyer's mind.

This mindset can translate into big wins for you if you can harness it right after new members join. It can and should be built right into your membership sales process timeline. I would recommend you formally ask your new members to provide referral names and contact information at some point during their orientation. Make sure it adds value for them. For instance, you could have some invitations to a complimentary round of golf or dinner ready to simply be addressed to their colleagues. The orientation process is a time that there should be a ton of excitement and expectation in the mind of your new member.

After events or tournaments at the club, I recommend to my clients that they survey the attendees. While this is important to gauge member satisfaction in and of itself, it's also a great time to ask members for referrals if the event was a success. It's that same concept in action. If they loved the event, they are in the perfect emotional state to tell others about the great times and the fun they have at their club.

Another time you should ask is when someone lets you know they are satisfied with their experience or offers a testimonial. This might happen in the form of a comment card, an email, a phone call, a social media post, etc. However it happens, don't just say you're happy to hear about it, make sure you use that opportunity to ask for the referral.

Recently I had a guest who appeared on the *Private Club Radio* Show email me to tell me that they closed a multi-million dollar deal as a direct result of appearing on my show. Apparently a board member of a prestigious club heard the interview and decided his club could use this guest's services. I was genuinely honored and excited to hear that, and I thanked that guest for letting me know. Rather than leaving it at that, I went on to tell them that they should consider a sponsorship of the show so that more people could hear them on a regular basis. I also attached some information about my sponsorship packages and asked them to take a look and see if it made sense. It was a genuine, no-pressure approach. It didn't take much deliberation. They signed up to be show sponsor right away because they recognized the value they had already received and wanted more. Take that same approach when members sing your praises and you're going to start seeing your leads by referral pile up.

INCENTIVIZING & GAMIFICATION

Humans are wired to compete and competition is in the DNA of private clubs. Golf, tennis, croquet, billiards and every other sport that's played in our clubs is played to win. There's a reason the member guest tournament is the most well attended event of the year at many clubs. That's why gamification is a powerful way to get your members referring. Gamification is simply the process of setting rules and giving people a goal or task in exchange for a reward.

When you were a kid did you ever go to an ice cream store and get that punch card where you buy 9 ice creams and get the 10th one free? If you answered yes, then you've been gamified! If you have ever participated in a frequent flyer program in hopes of getting a free ticket, you've played the airline's version of a game. In fact, when you play the airline's game for long enough, it's not even about the free ticket anymore, it's about the status and being able to say you are Platinum Elite Club Super Member of the Millennium, or whatever they're calling it now. That's why it's quite possibly the greatest of them all.

Games play to our most base desires as humans and that's why they work. The natural desire for praise and accolades from peers can be served by earning badges and gold stars that can be put on display. The innate need for exploration can be accomplished by things like scavenger hunts. The inborn thirst to win is quenched by point systems and a leaderboard. The inclination to stretch beyond ourselves is reached by completing challenges and attaining new levels. All this and more is achieved with gamification.

One way you can turn the referral process into a game is by setting up some sort of visual in a conspicuous place in the club. Get creative and make sure it's something that has to do with your club's brand. For instance, Tampa is big on pirates. We have an annual pirate festival called The Gasparilla Pirate Festival and our football team is the Buccaneers. Here in Tampa, I've helped clubs set up games like treasure maps complete with gold doubloons. For every member who was referred the referring member was rewarded with a coin hung on the wall with their name. The one who collected the most coins won the treasure - an all-expenses paid trip to an exclusive destination. Sure, it was a little corny, but it worked! I encourage you to think about some ways you can gamify the referral process at your club.

NETWORKING

If you're sitting behind a desk and hoping members will walk through the door, you're missing out on a wide world of opportunity. Beyond that, the more you sit around, the more the world will change and pass you by. In order to be the best you can be you've got to get out of your comfort zone, explore new opportunities and meet new people. I truly believe that as a business person (and that is what you are) you are only as good as your network. Strong networks lead to more members. In fact, what membership is at its core is simply a glorified form of networking.

Joining and being active in your community's chamber of commerce is one of the simplest things you can do to start building a more robust and strategic network. Not only are chambers of commerce frequented by the business owners and decision makers in town, those who attend have their own spheres of influence and further reaching networks as well. Most good chambers survive on the referral process themselves. If you can meet the influential folks in your community and help them, they will in turn help you.

Apart from the chamber of commerce, there are probably other local business associations in your community. These may be local chapters of larger networking organizations or there may be independent groups formed to serve a need. In either case, it's worth a couple of trips to see if it's a good mix of people. There are going to be some duds out there, but there are also going to be some honey holes.

Local realtor organizations are another great place to network and expand your own influence. If you're in a gated community and rely on home sales to drive membership, this is a no brainer. But even if you're not, realtors are the ones who are the first touch point for new families moving into the community. Folks from out of town often rely on their realtor to advise them on what's worthwhile to do and see. Being entrenched in this network will put you at the top of mind for this group.

Your local tourism authority would be a good next stop. These organizations often host mixers and other community events. Getting involved with the tourism authority and those associated with it can pay dividends in many ways. Firstly, other businesses may end up being a good referral source for you. Secondly, most tourism authorities do a lot of advertising, be it on websites, in magazines and/or on television. If you can get included in their campaigns, it will give you the same exposure without the big cash outlay.

My advice is to avoid attending any networking functions with the sole purpose of handing your business card to everyone who you meet. I see this happen a lot and it's a turnoff. People who do this are viewed by other attendees as interrupters trying to push their own agenda. It's a bad look.

Instead, take this approach. Focus on a few key people at each event and try to start a deeper and more meaningful conversation with them. Ask them thoughtful questions and be genuinely interested in them. Just the simple act of listening and paying attention makes you a great conversationalist in people's eyes. They only want to hear themselves most of the time anyway.

Approach each interaction as if you are looking to find *them* a referral. Don't just fake it either. Really do it! If you give someone else an introduction, most good networkers will feel obligated to repay the favor, often many times over. In networking, as in any relationship, you should first look to add value in someone's else's life. When you do that, you'll be rewarded.

DIRECT MAIL

One man's trash is another man's treasure. The old adage rings true when it comes to direct mail. So many people are stuck on the notion that "print is dead." Because of this, they forget about direct mail. Since so many people forget, people get less mail and consequently direct mail is alive and well. Funny how that works. Marketers often get sucked into the new fads and forget about the old tactics. The fact is, direct mail works well when done right.

The success of any direct mail campaign lies solely on the following factors: how good your list data is, how eye catching the mail piece is, and how compelling the offer is. Let's break them down one by one.

Mailing lists come in all shapes and sizes. At my agency, we have over 300 demographic and psychographic profiles that can be selected. In fact I've once boasted that we could find left-handed golfers in California who are vegetarians. How's that for granular detail? Now, of course, the more detail you request and the deeper you go, the more expensive that list gets.

When I'm working with a private club, I generally like to pull a list based on a few factors I've found consistently work. First of all, I'll select a radius within the average drive time of the club. Secondly, I pull income range based on the average income of members at the club. I pull an age range of a 10-year spread from the club's average. So if the average age of the club is 54, we go from 49-59. I also like to make sure the prospects have a golf, tennis or other interest related to what the club provides. If it's a yacht club for example, we pull a select for boating. With these four criteria I can get a much more targeted list. By the way, can you see why the KPIs we discussed earlier come in handy?

Now depending on the offer, we might go a little deeper. For instance, if it's a family oriented club and they are pushing the wonderful new summer camps they're providing their members, we might look for the presence of children in the home. As your offer gets more specific so too can the data.

Once you've got a solid list, that's half the battle. The next thing to do is make sure your creative really sizzles. Stay away from nondescript plain white number 10 envelopes. People throw those out because they look like bills or junk mail. Most times, I'll suggest postcards to my clients. The reason is because postcards can't be missed. Something oversized, glossy and colorful will stand out. At a minimum, a 6x9 postcard will do the trick, but you can go to 8.5x11 and larger as well. If you do go the envelope route, never do a standard number 10 envelope. Go with something like a 9x12. The first goal of direct mail is to actually get them to open or read it. You do that by standing out from the rest of what they're seeing.

The only time I wouldn't suggest a postcard or eye-catching full color envelope is when I'm dealing with ultra-exclusive high-end offers. For those, you'll want a little more modesty in the design. However, this is when your paper selection will be critical. You'll want something that feels luxurious, whether that's a silk or velvet texture or some type of patterned paper. You might also consider adding foil or embossing too. I'd be aiming for a $5 per piece range or so with something like this as opposed to postcards which will probably be in the $1 per piece range.

MASS MEDIA

Mass media, things like television, radio, billboards and publications, are going to generally be your least targeted approach when it comes to traditional marketing methods. This, however, should not necessarily dissuade you from their use. You just have to wade into the deep end a little more carefully and be prepared for a longer amount of time before you see results. In fact, I like my clients to think of mass media as more of a branding play. It shouldn't be a quick fix to your membership problem, but a long term strategy for staying relevant and top of mind in the eyes of the community.

Local publications are often the first form of marketing that clubs use. In this mix I would include things like newspapers, local or regional magazines, and weekend papers. Each publication should be able to provide you with a readership profile. Never place an ad in a publication without first reviewing this data. Without it, you're flying blind. This document should tell you the average age, income and other key demographics of their readership. Make sure it aligns with your own KPIs that you've been tracking.

Bonus Hack: One often underutilized tactic is getting your events listed in the weekend section or "things to do" section of your local paper and weekend publications. In

Tampa, where I'm from, Creative Loafing is the name of one of them and they are in many major US cities. While member-only events should stay private, things like open houses and invitations to the public should be published here if your club is holding such events. It's free advertising, so why not take the time to send a notice in? Beyond that, if published online there's a good chance you can get a link to your website on the listing. This is called a backlink and it's a good thing for the search engine optimization (SEO) of your website to have that link from a trusted source like a newspaper or publication. One way to ensure you get a link from the publication's website is to create a landing page for the registration and signups on your site. Make that the call to action in the listing.

Another thing to consider when you decide to place an ad in a mass media outlet is the run length, whether it be for a number of months, episodes or issues. You can't run an ad in a magazine one time and expect your phone to be ringing off the hook. You also can't put up a billboard for one month and expect a significant return on your investment. It just doesn't work that way. There's no hard and fast rule but you're going to need to be in it for the long haul. Repetition is the key to success with these marketing channels. Big brands know this and they have huge budgets. They buy billboard space for a year or more, they place ads and run commercials often. You may not be able to do that, which is why you should think long and hard before going this direction. Make sure it aligns with a long-term strategy. It might be a fit, and it might not.

When it comes to billboards and other outdoor advertising I want to offer you a special piece of advice. Make sure to keep your message clear and concise. My general rule is to keep your message to seven words or less. This includes the name of your club, by the way.

People's attention spans are shorter than ever today. In fact, a recent study showed that human attention spans have dwindled down to a mere eight seconds. That's less than a goldfish! Poorly executed billboards are complicated. They have offers, taglines and multiple calls to action —they list phone numbers, website addresses and the full address of the property sometimes. Who is going to write down an address while they're driving? Even passengers could quickly Google you on their smartphone and get the directions in the maps application! Those will only be perceived as clutter by folks driving by at 70 miles an hour. Don't make that mistake. On your next commute have a look at the billboards that catch your attention. I would wager that the vast majority of good ones are going to fall within a five to seven word limit.

With radio and television, you have 30 seconds and in some cases 15 to get someone's attention and get them to move to action. We talked earlier in this book about focusing on the emotional aspects of your offering, rather than the logical reasons to join your club. This is important when it comes to such a short frame. People can't digest a list of features in 30 seconds. However they can get a sense of what you are about and what type of lifestyle they can hope to enjoy.

People are attracted to people. So make sure you include people in the photography and video you use whenever possible. There's nothing more boring than a shot of a table setting or an empty golf course or bar. Put some people in there! Drone footage is great, but 30 seconds of flyovers are going to put people to sleep. No matter how spectacular your course design is, it's still grass, sand, trees and water.

If you don't have the budget to hire models and actors for your shots, a good graphic designer can add them in for you. Ask them to get some good stock images and cut them out to place in the scene. This is simple to do and adds dimension and life to otherwise static and un-memorable shots. There's a reason architects put people in their models of new buildings they design - so you can feel what it's like, and imagine yourself there. The same goes for advertising.

The last point I want to make about traditional media is that insertion prices and airtime are always negotiable. A media outlet sales rep may hand you his basic rate sheet, but they will always have some room to work with. At a minimum you should be able to negotiate a 10% discount and oftentimes it can be much more. It will depend on your negotiating skills and how desperate the salesperson is. The end of a month or sales period may often be your best bet to close a favorable deal because they are trying to hit a particular goal and your buy might push them over the top.

You may also want to consider hiring an agency to represent you. They will probably be able to negotiate even lower prices than you can, because of their buying power in representing multiple accounts. They'll receive a commission, usually 10%, but this will not affect your price and you'll have the added benefit of not having to deal with the negotiation process.

COLLATERAL MATERIALS

The most often used form of traditional marketing is collateral materials. These are business cards, brochures and other printed materials that the club has produced. Some clubs use their own newsletters or magazines as a form of soft advertising to the public and that is a great use of it.

What's important to consider with these types of materials is consistency. Everything that the club distributes needs to have a common aesthetic theme, a consistent color palette, font usage and paper type. When you lack consistency, it undermines your club's brand in a subtle yet very powerful psychological way.

I like to use the example of a steak dinner when I describe the importance of consistency. If you were to walk into a club's restaurant and order a beautiful USDA Prime New York strip cooked at a medium temperature and it came back rare you'd be disappointed. You would probably send it back, be a little irked, but as long as it came back good the second time you'd give it another shot. However, if the next time you went to the restaurant and ordered that medium steak only to find it came out well done, you wouldn't know what to expect. You'd probably never order it again. You'd assume the kitchen didn't know how to cook a proper steak. It's that lack of consistency that causes a lack of expectation that erodes your trust. On the other hand, if you were to walk into your club's dining room night after night, order the same steak, and have it perfectly cooked each time, you'd be a happy diner. You'd have an expectation that is continually met and it would form a psychological trust factor for the chef and the restaurant.

That's why consistency is so important and something that should never be overlooked. The best brands, be it Coca Cola, Apple, Rolex rely on consistency in their message and their aesthetic. If you see the Coca Cola red you could probably recognize it without even the logo there. That's how consistent they've been.

If your club is marketing without a brand standards manual, put this book down right now and get to work on one with a competent designer. This is not a job that should be left up to a staff member; you'll need to hire a professional. Your brand standards guide should include at a minimum acceptable and unacceptable logo usages, brand colors with corresponding CMYK, RGB and Pantone® (if applicable) values, as well as specific typefaces (fonts) that should be used. More detailed guides will show things like email signatures, letterheads, PowerPoint slide templates, paper types and other standard items that should stay consistent. This guide can grow as your needs arise. It should be given to anyone who creates something for your club whether that's a member, staff or outside designers and printers.

DIGITAL MARKETING STRATEGY

In this section we are going to cover digital marketing strategies. In broad terms this is any marketing that is done in an online environment. We'll be covering things like websites, pay per click ads, email marketing, social media marketing and other emerging trends that you should be aware of. The great thing about digital marketing is you have much more control, can get more accurate and quantifiable data and it's often much less expensive to implement and test strategy.

SOCIAL MEDIA

I want to start here because it's the strategy that can give you the most bang for your buck, but it's also the most misunderstood and misused. I see clubs do social media wrong every day. They post things that no one is interested in, they use language that doesn't resonate with the audience, they oversell and they miss out on opportunities that are all around. In this section, I'm hopefully going to help you change that.

THE IMPORTANCE OF SOCIAL LISTENING

Regardless of which of the following social media platforms you utilize, you should always engage in active social listening. Social listening is an under-utilized tactic for membership marketers. Too many clubs post online, but don't listen. You need to remember that the same rules apply for social networking as in-person networking. You have two ears and one mouth and should use them proportionally. So if you're not regularly scanning review sites or monitoring what people are saying about your club on social media you're missing some huge opportunities.

Not only should social listening be used for reputation management and addressing concerns that people describe, it should also be used for referral mining. Look for members who are extolling your club's virtues and make sure you communicate directly with them to give them some tools to refer. For instance, send those folks your digital brochure and ask those brand champions to send it to five folks they think could be potential members. By the way, it's important to give them a definitive number like five. That will give them some psychological motivation to complete the task and consider who realistically could become a good candidate for membership. Better yet, give them something like a "referral code" that's uniquely theirs. That way, they'll know you are tracking the results and can give them proper credit.

A great tool for social listening on Twitter is called TweetDeck. Go ahead and Google it. This site will let you see and respond in real time to all the comments that people make about your club. It's incredibly powerful. Make sure you search for both hashtags like "#yourclubname" and simply the name of your club spelled out like "your club name". You'll probably get results for both. Make sure to not only respond within the social media platform to keep the conversation going, but also private message these folks, thank them and ask for the referral.

On Instagram, I recommend you use a location search. Just type your club's name into the search box on their app, and you'll most likely see some results related to your club. This will be photos that people have taken at or near your property. If they are members, private message them or get their attention next time they are at the club.

As a bonus, you might get guests who have visited your club then snapped a photo or sent a tweet talking about their experience. If it was positive, share that post, then follow up. Now you've got yourself a few new hot leads!

CHOOSING A VOICE AND A PLATFORM

Whether you're just beginning your club's social media account or you're in the process of reinventing it, it's going to be important to first decide on a "voice" before you start. Creating this "voice" will give you a firm foundation and a roadmap of how and when to interact online. If multiple people are managing the account, it will help you stay consistent and on-message. It will also make you memorable and relatable, which is the most important part of social media strategy.

What is a "voice" you ask? The best way I can describe it is by calling it your brand's personality. Whether you want to sound prestigious, family friendly, approachable, entertaining, or a myriad of other things, these are all achieved by the tone and word choice in your communications. If you are trying to decide which voice direction to take and you do have some post history, go back and see what people connected with. What did they share or like or comment on? Many social media platforms offer page analytics that give you a snapshot of your most engaging and least engaging posts. See if you can recognize a pattern. If you don't have this, you'll just have to take the leap based on what you know of your club's established culture.

While there's no right or wrong approach when it comes to choosing a tone, there are a few that I don't think will work very well for private clubs. Those include the snarky/sarcastic tone, the melodramatic tone, the negative tone, and more. The snarky voice may be entertaining and work for other brands like Taco Bell or Wendy's, but they are catering to a completely different clientele. Whatever you choose, it should be in line with your club's values and mission. That's the best place to start.

Once you've decided on the right tone, you'll then need to decide which social networks to participate in. At a minimum, I advise clubs to try Facebook and LinkedIn. For clubs that are a little more comfortable, I'll tell them to add Instagram, Twitter and Pinterest. In general I'll advise against Google Plus, Snapchat and other more fringe networks.

It's important to treat each network differently. Many times, people think they can post the same thing on every network and be more productive. Social media doesn't work that way because each network has its own rules, both informal and formal. Each network also hits a slightly different demographic, and meets different needs within that demographic in terms of information delivery. When people take the one-size-fits-all approach users see right through it and tune out. While tools like Hootsuite allow you to post across all your social networks at once, I'd advise that you tweak your message for each. Hootsuite is a great time saving tool and should be used, but it shouldn't be a crutch to lean on for this lazy approach.

WHAT PEOPLE ENGAGE WITH ON SOCIAL MEDIA

So what do people actually want when it comes to their social media experience? It can all be boiled down to one thing: People want to hear a story. Since the dawn of humankind, our ancestors have sat around campfires telling tales and fables and reciting histories. Deep within each of us is a desire to connect with others, and the narrative is our most useful tool to accomplishing that end. Your job as a social media marketer should be to find and tell great stories. If you take this approach you'll never go wrong. The following are a couple of examples of how you can turn a boring post into a great story.

My friend Marc Ensign is a captivating storyteller. He has given talks around the country to massive audiences and wows them time after time with his stories. I asked him to share some advice when it comes to crafting a story. "Most companies tell their story by cramming as many impressive facts (that most people don't care about) into a wall of text," he said. "It's the equivalent of wearing all of your jewelry at one time. It looks ridiculous and nobody is impressed. What most people really care about is why you do what you do and what you went through to get there. People want to root for the underdog. The impossible journey. Which is ironic because most of those struggles are the things that companies hide because they are afraid of looking bad."

Here's an example of how this could work in practice. The next time you're tempted to post the results of your member/member tournament don't just simply list the winners and their respective scores with a picture of them holding the trophy. Instead tell your followers how Mr. Jones hit his tee shot into the woods, was nearly stymied but hit an incredible fade that wrapped around the trees, sailed just over the bunker and landed three feet away for an easy birdie to win out by one stroke. That's a remarkable story, and one that makes the win relatable to a wide audience.

Instead of telling people that there's a new off-season membership category to preview the club, instead show them photos of all the things they'll be doing during their three-month trial membership. Show them pictures of people enjoying the pool, laughing over drinks and hitting tennis shots at dusk. Make it the story of a day in the life a member. That's something people can engage in. It puts them in the moment.

Rather than showing a picture of a table setting for a wedding and letting people know that they should book their next event at the club, have one of the brides who have been married at the club tell the story of their wedding day and how perfect and befitting of a storybook it felt.

These are just a couple of ideas but I think by now you get my point. This type of content that is told in narrative form is immersive and sharable. It's not a sales pitch or a status update, but something much richer and more intriguing.

FACEBOOK

Facebook is the most influential and far reaching social network that has ever come into existence. Facebook has also done an incredible job of building psychographic profiles of their users. Every time a user engages, likes or shares something on Facebook, the platform is storing that information and building a profile of that individual. It uses that information to decide what that user will see each time they log in. For me, Facebook has the potential to be *the* most powerful marketing platform ever invented.

The problem is, not many people have taken a look under the hood.

FACEBOOK PAGES

A Facebook page is a must, in my opinion, for any club. With members from all generations active on Facebook, you've got to be there to be relevant and stay top of mind. Most clubs use Facebook to simply update their members on events happening around the club. That's all well and good if your membership is capped and you have a deep waiting list to get into your club. Most clubs aren't in that boat, however. If your club is one that is looking for members, your posts had better stand out from the ordinary (within reason of course). They had better delight, inform and entertain because then they will appeal to a broader audience.

Everything you post on a public page in Facebook has the potential to be seen outside your membership, so every post should be engaging and offer a benefit to the reader. I often encourage my clients to post tips, tricks and useful advice. Things like the golf tip of the day or the wine pairing of the month will get people coming back to your page often, and will also create shareable opportunities, thereby expanding your club's reach to people within that member's circle of friends. Think of a few outside the box things you could start posting on a consistent basis. You'll see a dramatic difference in engagement once you begin doing it.

FACEBOOK ADS CHANGED THE GAME

When Facebook decided to launch its advertising platform, it was both a benefit and a curse. Overnight, pages that had hundreds or even thousands of followers soon began to reach only a fraction of that number when they posted. 10% or less of those who liked the page were served the post in their newsfeed. This is great for users because they are served only the most relevant information, thus de-cluttering their news feeds, but it also makes it difficult for pages to have their posts seen. You have to realize not every post is going to be seen by everyone, but there are some tips I can give you to help you reach the maximum amount of users.

The success or failure of your post is heavily reliant on the engagement it receives in the first few minutes of it going live. Facebook's algorithm determines how relevant your post is based on who likes, comments or shares when they see it come across their feed. If more people take those actions right away, it will be served to others. If they don't it will be buried in the abyss never to be seen again, unless you pay to boost it (more on that later).

I've found that time of day plays a big role in whether or not people will see it and engage. The posts that get the most engagement are made in the morning, around 7:00 am to 8:00 am and in the early evening from 4:30 pm to 6:30 pm. This is prime time for Facebook. I can only assume this is because people are checking it before and after work when they're not interacting with their family and friends in a "live" environment. When I post during these times, my content gains momentum quicker than if I was to post midday, early morning or late evening.

If there is a post that you really want to gain some traction with, make sure you give people notice ahead of time to like and share it. This will ensure it gets the most reach it possibly can. Ask your colleagues, members and even friends and family who follow the page to share it. You can also tag some key individuals in the comments section to elicit some reactions. While this shouldn't be done too often, it's a good tactic to get your post in front of some extra eyeballs.

The last thing I want to mention is that if you want people to interact with your posts, you'll need to be conversational. Asking a question or taking an informal poll is one of the most powerful ways to get your audience involved. When I ask a question on Facebook, I'll get double or triple the comments I normally do. People like to share their opinion, so give them every opportunity to and you'll see it pays off.

People also like the personal touch. Whenever possible, respond to their comments with their name in your reply. Something like, "Glad to hear you enjoyed the tournament, Lisa," lets your audience feel like they are special, rather than just another number. Just liking a comment and moving on robs you of a valuable opportunity to increase good will, raise engagement and create more of an emotional connection between your members and your club.

FACEBOOK AD STRATEGY

While standard posts are how most people use Facebook, the real power lies in Facebook ads. As I mentioned, our big blue brother has collected the most comprehensive data set on the human population since the dawn of mankind. This allows for hyper targeting on an epic scale. There is a seemingly endless set of criteria that you can narrow your focus on. Just like direct mail, you can choose a radius from your zip code, age, occupation and the most comprehensive set of affinities and hobbies ever gathered.

What's great about Facebook ads is that they are, at the time of this writing, extremely cheap compared to other marketing channels. I run campaigns for my clients that are often one-fifth of the price of things like Google Adwords, which we'll discuss later. I regular pay well under $1 for traffic from extremely targeted users. which is a dirt cheap cost per click (CPC). The value of Facebook is truly unmatched in the digital space.

To add another layer, Facebook has created something it calls Custom Audiences. This allows you to target people who have already interacted with you in some way. For instance, you can target folks who have visited your website, even those who have visited a specific page on your website—let's say the tennis page. In a case like that, you can then serve those people an ad specific to tennis. How cool is that?

In addition, you can feed the Custom Audiences application your own list of prospects and as long as you have their telephones or emails or both, Facebook will match them. The reason is, people are required to log into Facebook with either their email or phone. In my use cases, it matched approximately 40% of the lists I fed it, on average. That's very powerful because you've probably made contact with them in another way before finding them on Facebook. So this will be at least the second time you've made contact. Your message is more likely to break through and get noticed because you've already got some recognition.

If you want to go deeper still you can do something Facebook calls Lookalike Audiences. What this does is take your existing audience and analyzes what those folks have in common with other Facebook users, whether that's things they liked or commented on or pages they visited. It then targets those new users it found with your ads. To me, this is incredible. It takes the guesswork out of digital marketing.

There are many other ways to build custom audiences but I think this should be enough to keep you busy to begin with. As you get more comfortable you can get even more granular.

Once you've got your audience you can set your own budget. Facebook allows you to tell it how much you will pay for a view of for a click, or you can let Facebook decide for you. From experience, I'd recommend the latter. It seems to work better and more efficiently. Facebook will optimize who it serves your ad to, what time of day and more. It works remarkably well on its own.

You can set a daily limit or choose a budget for the month. You can also set a lifetime budget for the campaign. I'd recommend spending at least $250 per month to begin with and testing this strategy for at least 3 months. This works out to a little over $8 per day. It's a good start to get your feet wet and work out the kinks. And don't forget to run a few different versions to test what works best. Facebook allows you to have multiple ads within your campaign which allows you to split test and see what's working and what's not. That's the great thing about digital; it is inexpensive enough to let you do some testing. Like anything else, it's not an exact science, so you'll have to see what works best for you and continually tweak your campaigns to get the best results.

All of this can seem overwhelming to beginning marketers. So if this is your first foray into the world of pay per click advertising, it's probably best you seek guidance from an expert. It also makes sense to retain an agency if you are running multiple campaigns or if this is only a part of your digital strategy. Most will charge a nominal monthly management fee, take care of all the targeting, budgeting and tweaking and provide you with detailed monthly reporting. This will help you stay focused on the big picture and not get caught up in the minutia.

LINKEDIN

The next social network worth spending your time on is LinkedIn. As you probably know, LinkedIn is much more business focused than Facebook. That means no shots of your kids, what you had to eat for dinner or your latest vacation. People on LinkedIn are searching for ideas, best practices and professional connections. Your posts should focus on these things pretty narrowly. Every once in a while it will be good to share some personality, but make sure you're still providing value first.

While you can and should have some type of business profile setup for the club, the real power in LinkedIn will be your personal page. I know for some this might seem uncomfortable, but I think once you get your feet wet you'll really enjoy it.

LinkedIn can be a powerful tool for prospecting. It also has some hidden features that might surprise you. I'm going to show you a few helpful hacks to use LinkedIn a little more effectively than just posting your resume and sharing articles you find on the internet.

The coolest thing that LinkedIn can do, in my opinion, is generate a list of prospect's email addresses. Just like Facebook, LinkedIn requires users to sign in with their email. When you connect with someone, you then have access to see that person's email address. I don't know of any other social network that does this.

Here's how you can export email addresses from your network on LinkedIn. Please exercise some discretion with this, and please note these are the instructions as of the writing of this book. Login to your LinkedIn account and up at the top of the page hover over the menu item labeled "My Network". A drop down menu will appear and you can select "Connections". From there it will open up a new page that will show you how many connections you have and list them. Ignore all that and look for the gear icon in the top right of the page. When you click that you'll open another page that will show you some useful things you can do. On the right hand sidebar you'll see a folder icon with a downward pointing arrow labeled "export LinkedIn connections". Click that and you'll be taken to a download page. I'd recommend choosing the .csv file format for export, which will then be importable into CRMs or mailing programs. That will generate and download a nicely formatted list for you complete with company information, job title and more. Just weed out the people who are colleagues and friends and you've now got a solid list to prospect with. Work on building those connections and growing that list and do this often.

Once you have that list, you can use it to find and target people on Facebook using the retargeting method I described earlier. Remember, it's always important to reach people in multiple ways on multiple platforms. With this, you're connected on LinkedIn, via email, and potentially connected with Facebook as long as they use the same email address. That cross-platform connectedness makes your message that much more likely to stick.

Another great hidden feature of LinkedIn is something they call "Advanced Search". By using this feature you can look for connections to add by narrowing your focus down to certain companies, certain occupations, schools they have attended and more. LinkedIn will perform the search and give you some leads to consider connecting with. What's better, you can save that search so that LinkedIn will automatically send you new suggestions weekly or monthly. That automation will save you valuable time.

There are so many fun things you can do with LinkedIn it could fill its own book, but I'll leave you with one last tip that you might find useful. When you are prospecting and searching for folks to connect with that might be potential club members it's probably helpful to know if they are into golf or tennis or the activities that your club provides. With LinkedIn, you can find out about the interests of your potential connections right from their profile page. Simply click on the profile of someone you're thinking of connecting with. When it's someone you're not already connected with, there will be a big blue button in the middle of the page to the right of their picture that says "Connect" and next to that another grey button asking to "Send InMail". If you click on the little arrow drop-down icon, you'll get some more options. From there you can choose "View recent activity". That will allow you to see what they've shared, liked and commented on. If you find there are a lot of things like golf, tennis, yachting or whatever your club offers, you've found yourself a very likely candidate.

By using these three built-in features of LinkedIn, you'll be able to make your social networking much more productive. Happy prospecting! And don't forget, LinkedIn is a powerful way to find top talent, too. If you're a manager looking to hire, make sure you check your candidates' profiles out. You may be able to weed out some bad apples or recognize some new strengths.

INSTAGRAM

Instagram is a photo and video sharing network only, but it's extremely powerful. If you want to reach millennials and Gen X'ers this is a network you should target in particular. It's owned by Facebook so there is some extra connectivity and some useful tools built in to make it a little more intuitive than you can find with similar networks like SnapChat.

Instagram lends itself to storytelling better than any other social network in my opinion. By taking multiple shots throughout an event like a wedding, golf tournament or wine tasting night you can build a nice picture of what it was like to be there and experience it. It can be used as an album for just about any activity that your club provides. It's fun and really easy to learn. I know you're not concerned with the fun factor though and want tips on how it can be used to effectively market membership. So let's get into a few of my Instagram hacks.

First off, hashtagging is used heavily on Instagram for people to discover things that they are interested in. If you're not familiar with the term, these are the hash signs that look like "#" followed by a word or phrase. Unlike Twitter, hash tags can be used without a character limit. Often you'll see photos with 10 or 20 or more hashtags being used and that's ok in terms of etiquette on the network. Since your club is most likely looking for local prospects, you should localize the hashtags you use. Things like #golftampa or #tampawedding would be more useful than just saying #golf or #wedding for instance. Make sure you look at how often the hashtags are used. Instagram will tell you this as you're typing it, so you'll know if it's a keyword people are interested in. Please avoid the temptation of making up your own random hashtag like #besthartruten-niscourtsinwherever. No one will search that so you'll just be wasting space and cluttering your message. By using hashtags properly you'll attract followers and onlookers. It will almost feel like magic.

The next most important way to use Instagram is to use their location identifier. Within the Instagram app, you can search for photos by location. This is powerful in a couple of different ways. First you can use it to see who's talking about your club. This is also a way to monitor your club's own reputation on Instagram. If people are saying things, good or bad, it's worthwhile for you to respond to those comments. You might also find some problems that need to be fixed or good things that should be focused on. The other way you can use location searches is to find others in your local community who could be potential prospects for your club. If there's a guy who takes shots of his Rolex watches while golfing or sipping high end bottles of wine at local restaurants, there's a good chance he's a candidate for membership at your club. He's got the money and the taste for what your club has to offer.

The newest feature of Instragram is what they are calling "Your Story". Your story is a SnapChat style storyline of your day. You take photos throughout the day, add them to Your Story, and you can create a narrative. You can also use these same photos on Facebook, in their new collage option for photos. This is a good place to pitch what your club has to offer. Get people wrapped up in the story of a day in the life of your club for instance, and then invite them for a VIP tour. I think this can be a real winner but it will take some trial and error on your part to figure out the best approach. Like anything else, don't be afraid to test out new ways to engage and don't be afraid to fail. There's always a lesson to learn.

TWITTER

Twitter is all about quick and easy to digest information. Twitter is probably the hardest network to form a narrative on because of the character limitation it imposes. This makes it fun, but it also makes it hard to elaborate. It's better if you use Twitter for facts, tips, news and announcements. As such, I've found it's hard for clubs to have a whole lot of success on this platform, by solely posting. However, what Twitter really excels at is search.

Early on, Twitter developed a way to index the topics that its users were tweeting about. They did this with the hashtag. They then developed something called trending topics which would track which hashtags were being used most frequently. Today every word is indexed whether it's hashtagged or not. This makes it incredibly powerful as a search tool to find out what people are saying about your club and within the vicinity of your club. This is really the way that I recommend Twitter be utilized. It's much more strategic.

You can also search those hashtags on Twitter, see how many people are responding or commenting using that term, and then use that to target your tweets and your Instagram posts.

One tool that will make these efforts a breeze is TweetDeck. TweetDeck is a separate website from Twitter but it's owned by them. If you are using or want to use Twitter for your club, I think this is an essential tool. It's free and will help your prospecting and social listening efforts immensely.

The way TweetDeck works is that you set up feeds to monitor particular keywords, phrases and hashtags. For example, you could choose to follow "golf tampa", "golfing in tampa", "#golftampa", and "Tampa Country Club" all simultaneously. By doing so you'll be able to see streams of folks in real-time who are having conversations and asking questions related to subjects relevant to your club.

The key is this is happening in real time. That means you can hop in and respond in real time too! If you're going to win at Twitter, it's vital to take this approach. No one cares about a reply, an answer or a retweet weeks later. Twitter is fast and caters to the on-demand individual. If you don't answer that day, you've lost someone's interest as they've moved on to a host of other topics.

Don't be afraid to try out new words and phrases and track them for a few days. If there's not much activity and no one is discussing those topics you can easily delete the feed and try something new. Anything related to your club or hashtags that you've developed specifically for use by members and guests should be tracked no matter how little they are used, however. You won't want to miss these as they come through.

I know that it may seem overwhelming to be glued to TweetDeck all day, but this is something you can check once or twice a day. It's also a good job for the club's receptionist or someone who has a bit of downtime throughout the day. They can check periodically and see if there's anything worth responding to.

One hack I have for you when it comes to Twitter and TweetDeck is to follow specific questions and to do so by using everyday words that people actually use. Many people are looking for advice on Twitter, and it's wise to follow these phrases. You should try out things like "looking for" or "need to" along with relevant keywords. An example would be, "looking for club tampa" or "need wedding tampa" (if you are actively trying to book outside events like weddings). Following these phrases allow you to jump in and offer up your services. Speed is the key, and many times the first to respond wins.

PINTEREST

Pinterest is another photo sharing site. However, unlike Instagram, most folks do not create their own photos, but rather grab images from around the web and create virtual "pinboards" for topics that interest them. For example, if you want to renovate your kitchen, you might find ideas from designers and kitchen concepts you've seen around the web and put them all in one place to help you choose design elements. If you want to elevate your cooking game you might collect recipes for great dishes from famous chefs. In this way, it's a great brainstorming and crowd-sourcing tool for folks.

With a business page for your club you can create and share content that others will find and interact with. This content creation along with curation will establish your club as a player in the community. You could setup pinboards for your wine collection or pairing notes, the golf course hole by hole, delicious chef specials, a poolside gallery and much more. Wedding pinboards are especially popular on Pinterest, so consider creating one of those for your club as well. People on Pinterest are searching for creative and relaxing escapes and this is a powerful way to attract those individuals. You'll get them when they're in the right frame of mind too.

So why should you consider this network? As of this book's writing, 30% of online adults in the United States use Pinterest and a whopping 85% of those are females.

This is a good thing because more and more women play an ever increasing role in a family's finances. They are often the ones making purchasing decisions. They'll certainly have a say at the very least. So if you're looking to attract the ladies of the household, you might just want to spend a little time on this network. Pinterest is also a haven for millennials. Over 30% of its users fall into this age group. If that's a demographic you're looking to target, Pinterest a good place to find them. Lastly, people on Pinterest are spenders. Users here spend four times more than those on Facebook and users spend 70% more money when they arrive at websites from links they clicked on Pinterest. That's the incredible power of curating ideas!

Many clubs allow outside events like weddings, business meetings and golf outings. I think this is good for clubs who are actively seeking members because it brings a couple of hundred new faces to your doors. If they are locals, that's great because they might see something they like or enjoy their time enough to pursue membership. If they are from out of town it's great, too. Those folks often snap a lot of pictures and share them on social media. That's free PR! For clubs that do allow these events, make sure to set up some pinboards about your wedding and catering services. Show folks that delicious food, those wonderful decorations and those magical moments. With a woman-dominated network, those tend to be re-pinned often.

Have some fun with this network and post often. For clubs that are less worried about exclusivity and privacy, go ahead and install "Pin It" on your website. This will allow users to share your content organically within the site. By doing that, they exponentially increase your reach online.

YOUTUBE

Video is a strategy that your club should not overlook. In the world of online video, YouTube is king. YouTube claims that they have over 1 billion users worldwide. That stat is incredible alone. What's more fascinating is that they reach more 18-34 year olds and 18-49 year olds with just their mobile platform than any cable network in the United States. After Google, who owns it, YouTube is the world's second largest search engine, handling over 3 billion searches per month. If you are ignoring YouTube in your digital marketing strategy, you're making a big mistake because it's where many new brands get discovered. With mobile technology getting advanced, you have a 4k movie production studio right on your phone. So there's not much excuse to not get involved.

Just like a blog, I suggest you create a strategy to constantly create video content on YouTube. Whether that's a video per week or per month, get in the habit of regularly making something new. Tips, tricks and tutorial videos are an easy place to start. Get your department heads together to brainstorm a few ideas that will excite and entertain not just your members, but golfers, tennis players, diners, sailors and folks who do business in your community.

Here are a few tips I can offer as you enter this new space with your club:

1. **Make sure that the majority of your videos are short and to the point**. In my opinion, two minutes or less is the best length for most online videos unless you are walking someone through something complicated like a cooking recipe.

2. **Don't neglect sound.** Sound is 50% of the video experience so invest in a microphone. Many can be had for $75 or less. It will improve your video quality dramatically.

3. **Make sure to write keyword rich headlines and descriptions.** As noted above, YouTube is basically a giant search engine. Make sure that you write captivating headlines that catch people's attention and are related to your subject. Don't make them vague. Also, write long descriptions of your videos and don't forget to link to your website. That will provide you some good SEO juice flowing back to your site.

4. **Stay consistent.** I know it's hard to do, but get on a schedule and post at a consistent interval. I'd suggest you create a content calendar and keep it near your desk. If you're lucky enough to build subscribers (YouTube's version of followers) they'll come back to see you at regular times. Don't let them be disappointed.

5. **Smile when you speak.** It's hard to do, but keep a grin on your face as you or your "star" is speaking. It feels unnatural, but it will come across much more personable on screen. Practice talking while holding a smile on your face in front of a mirror and you will see what I mean.

6. **Transcribe Videos.** By providing a transcription, you'll make your video much more findable in YouTube's search engine. The system is so advanced that it now creates automatic transcriptions; you'll just need to tweak them a little. It's very quick to do.

Pro Tip: Create your own hashtag on YouTube. By setting up a unique hashtag that no one else will use like #tampacountryclubtip, you can keep people within your own world. When a video ends on YouTube, it generally suggests similar videos. If all of your videos have the same hashtag, it will suggest your videos exclusively. This will keep people from getting distracted and leaving your channel.

LIVE STREAMING - A NEW FRONTIER

Very few clubs have ventured into the world of live streaming and I think that's a big missed opportunity. If you're unfamiliar with what live streaming is, it's live video that you broadcast openly to the world from your mobile device. People can find your feed, watch it and comment in real time on what you're experiencing or the story that you're telling.

Live streaming is the most powerful invention in the history of social networking and one of the most important advances in human history. I don't say this for melodramatic effect—I truly believe it. To put it in perspective, with live streaming you now have the ability to be your own television station and PR agency all in one. That's a game changer. This is an exciting time to be a social media marketer, because if you're an early adopter and can figure out a recipe for success, you'll have the potential to corner this new market.

Currently the world of live streaming is a little like the Wild West. Everyone is still trying to figure it out. At the time writing this book, it has really only been around for a little over a year. Networks have already popped up and fizzled out and new ones are emerging. There are two that I've told people they should focus on and those have proved to, so far, be correct. Those two are Periscope and Facebook Live. Periscope is owned by Twitter and Facebook Live is of course built right into Facebook, which means you can leverage the network you've already built.

It's scary to turn on your phone's camera for the first time and go live, but once you get the hang of it it's exhilarating. Almost magically, you'll see people begin to view it. The newest mobile update of Facebook alerts users of a new video posted by friends or pages they have liked. People can also search for live videos happening around them, by specific location, or within the network you've built. Then if you're entertaining enough, those people will share the link, and others from outside your network will begin to watch. People will then "like" and "comment" on what you're discussing. It's all organic and somewhat surreal, but most of all fun!

If you don't know where to start, that's ok. Here are a few things you can do to begin attracting and building an audience for your club:

The golf tip of the week: get your pro out on the driving range to share his best tip for improving your game.

The wine pairing of the month: Have your chef or sommelier teach the audience how to choose the right vintage.

Live tour of the club: Have your membership director or general manager take people on a virtual tour of the facilities.

History lesson from the president: Give members and non-members a monthly taste of the rich history your club.

Sailing lessons: Teach someone how to sail and you'll be top of mind when they want to join a yacht club.

The possibilities are only limited by your creativity. Don't be afraid to try things out and test new concepts. Remember people are looking for interesting things, ideas and advice. Provide that rich content and you'll be one of the most talked about and the most coveted experiences in town and maybe even around the world!

Beyond the marketing benefits, this is a great team building exercise. It's going to take at least two people to pull these vignettes off—the person behind the camera and the person in front of the camera. You may involve a team in the process. Keep these fun and lighthearted and watch your staff's morale increase, and your membership interact more.

SNAPCHAT, GOOGLE PLUS AND OTHERS

Lots of clubs ask me if they should be using another particular network. My advice is that if you can conquer the others I've previously mentioned, you'll have a much larger audience than the others would ever provide.

SnapChat is interesting but its vibe is not conducive to the club experience, in my opinion. For me it's clunky and the interface is not intuitive enough to be useful. It's also very difficult to find people and develop new connections. While some older generations are beginning to use it as well as some businesses, it's still a haven for a much younger audience. These things may change, but for now it's best to wait and see.

As for Google Plus, this is really a community that is more engaged in tech and current events. While you might find some success here, you'll likely get better results elsewhere in my experience. If you are going to use this network, the best use is to set up a community page, which is similar to a message board where folks post and interact, or a "collection", which is similar to a Pinterest pinboard.

As for emerging networks, my general advice is to stay away until they've been around for five years or more. That's a good test of a network's longevity. New, hot, must-try social networks pop up every few months. Most never gain traction from the mainstream and end up wasting your time as a marketer. That's a lost opportunity cost that could've been better spent on a more proven network. There are plenty of other marketers who are willing to test the waters and see if they're viable. In the private club industry I'm all for cutting edge, but bleeding edge isn't often worth the risk.

ORGANIC SEARCH

The results that Google and other search engines return which are not paid ads are called "organic results". The Holy Grail for websites is to be at the top spot when someone performs a search. The second page of search results is where clubs and other businesses go to die. Nobody, except the completely desperate, ever gets there. It can be argued that search engines, and Google in particular, are so advanced that this happens after the first couple results on the first page. When was the last time you went half way down to find what you were looking for?

My own website happens to be at the top spot for many search terms locally in Tampa where my business is located. If you were to search for "graphic design tampa" "graphic designers" and similar terms my company's site would be the first listing. Consequently, we get phone calls daily from people who are searching for design services.

My site didn't get to the top overnight. It took three or four solid years to do that, but all that work is now paying off in spades. We don't have to prospect, or spend money on advertising locally because leads come to us. I don't say this to brag, but to tell you that it is indeed possible without having to pay a search engine optimization company thousands of dollars each month.

A good friend of mine and fellow marketer, Chris Krimitsos, believes that getting to the top organically is going to be more important than ever. With the advent of software assistants like Apple's Siri and Amazon's Echo there will soon only be one result and that will be the one that is most relevant to the request. In a few years when everyone is asking their devices, "Siri, where is the best place to play golf?" or "Alexa, what's the best restaurant?" *you* had better be the answer. That will be a direct result of being the first search result. I believe he's one hundred percent right.

No matter what anyone tells you, search engine optimization is not rocket science and it's not magic. You don't need to game the system or do anything that is unethical. There are a few steps that your club can take, free of charge, which will get you moving up the ranks of the search engines. These include: content creation and curation, natural link building, and user reviews. Constantly developing these three elements will eventually land you at the top.

CONTENT CREATION AND CURATION

Most club websites are devoid of content. It's a holdover from a time when clubs believed that they were private and exclusive and should not let the general public in on the secret. We know those days are gone, yet the problem persists. I interviewed Jeff Morgan, CEO of the CMAA, about this lack of information on club websites and what he thought of it. His answer was, "I think that is an area that clubs have been traditionally shying away from, but as we open our doors up to the community it's a great way to tell the story [of the club]. It's something we can all do without a lot of extra expense." He went on to explain that telling the story of your club and its members isn't any different than what other businesses and community organizations do on their own sites. It's not necessarily advertising, it's telling a story. I think he hit the nail on the head.

Fresh, relevant content is what search engines are looking for. Google, in particular, wants to see websites that are expanding by adding regular new content and capturing visitors' attention. It measures this by how long a user stays on the site. There's no magic number to how much content you need to produce but it should be regular. I advise my clients to write a new article either weekly or at a minimum monthly. Get in the habit of putting out fresh info and create a content calendar.

At first glance, writing an article might have a few people scratching their heads. It might seem overwhelming amidst all of your other priorities. I totally understand. However, there's a good chance you're already creating some type of article or content and you can simply re-purpose it for your website. You might have articles that you put in your club's newsletter that can be used online, too. All of those social media posts can be expounded upon. Just like we touched on in the live streaming section, you might have a tennis or golf pro put out their tip of the week or month. This would be a wonderful way to repackage the same content in a few ways.

Another idea is simply content curation. There are great articles and videos all over the web that you can cite, write a few paragraphs of opinion on and link to. That process takes all of fifteen minutes once you get in the habit of doing it. Creating this news or knowledge base section on your website is the first and most important step in gaining traction with the search engines. If you absolutely hate writing, there are copywriters, freelancers and agencies that do this stuff day in and day out. You'll have to educate them on the type of content and the audience you're trying to serve, but most good ones will be able to consistently deliver you good content.

LINK BUILDING

After content creation, links in and out of your site are the next biggest determining factor for which sites are displayed at the top of search results. While outgoing links (links from your site out to other sites on the web) should be built, it's more important to have reputable sites linking to yours. The more reputable and influential the site, the more that incoming link signals to the search engine that you're important.

There was a noticeable uptick in my own website traffic when I was quoted on the *Entrepreneur Magazine*® website for instance. Because this site is trusted and read by millions around the world, their link to my website sent a strong signal to Google that my site was relevant.

A few years back, many marketers and SEO folks used to game the system by creating what was called link banks or link farms. Basically these were spammy websites that linked to all of their client's pages. Google has since recognized and banned this shady practice. Many people think that because this happened, links don't contribute to a site's SEO, but from experience I can tell you it's not the case.

Link building can be accomplished in a number of ways. Firstly, you can ask vendors or companies with whom your club has a relationship to place links on their site. Secondly, having staff, members, or the club as a whole, featured in the news will garner some strong links back. News sites often rank very well and their links are trusted by the search engines. Another tactic is to comment on blogs and other sites across the web related to things like golf, food and beverage, tennis, weddings and other activities that take place at the club. Most comment forms allow you to place a link back to your own site. It's low hanging fruit and takes very little time. Lastly don't forget to share intriguing content online with links back to your web pages. Search engines pick up on those social signals and that also improves your chances.

REVIEW SITES

Review sites like Yelp, Travelocity and Google Places aren't just important to your club's reputation, they are vitally important to letting search engines know about you. In fact, Google values its own reviews so much that they are now placed at the top or just below the top of the first page of results. And on top of that, often mixed within the first few results are other review sites! This is mostly due to the fact that their users are creating new content daily and they're linking to so many reputable sites. See how those first two steps I mentioned work?

I highly recommend you make every effort possible to encourage both members and guests of your club to write a review for you primarily on Google, and then on some of the other review sites as well. The easiest way is to direct them to search for your club on the Google maps phone application and enter the review there. Now, you don't want all the reviews to come in at once. That won't look natural to Google and they may penalize you for it. Instead, they should trickle in steadily each week or month.

Get creative on how you ask for reviews. On my site, when someone pays their invoice, the success message includes a direct link to my Google business page and asks them to leave a review. You might direct message someone on social media and ask them to do it. You could send a few emails to different folks each week. If you're providing a top-notch experience, most folks would be happy to take three minutes out of their day and write a quick five-star review.

MOBILE RESPONSIVE SITES

In 2017 as I write this, most club websites I browse are not mobile responsive. That is to say, they do not adjust their presentation for a mobile device like a phone or tablet. Users are still required to pinch and zoom in order read things on the page. To me this is shocking and a gross failure on the part of the industry's major players in the web building space.

The simple fact is if your website is not responsive you will be penalized by Google's algorithm so much that you'll have no chance of ever being on the first page of results. If your site looks the same on a desktop as it does on the phone, you're in this category and you should immediately get your developer on the phone or hire a new one. Desktop computers are soon to go the way of the dinosaur. Today, more people access the web from mobile devices than desktops. I will also add that having a "mobile version" of your site is not good enough either. It's often clunky and cheats your visitors out of a good browsing experience. The time is now to make the switch and improve your user's experience.

THE X CURVE

There's a good chance that if you're reading this you're starting from scratch. While you recognize the value of search engine optimization (SEO), you probably would like to build your membership now, not three years down the road. That's where the next section on using search engine marketing (SEM) is going to come in handy.

I like to think of SEO and SEM as interdependent. If you were to plot it out in graphical form, on one axis you would have SEO and on the other you have SEM. When you start out, you SEO, or organic search, is low and your SEM, or paid search, should be high. Over time they should move in opposite directions. Eventually your SEO will increase and your SEM should decline. It will look like an "X".

If you follow this method, there will be a healthy balance in creating your short-term and long-term strategy. Using SEM in the short term for the quick wins will give you the necessary capital and resources to invest in the sustainable long-term SEO strategy.

SEARCH ENGINE MARKETING AND GOOGLE ADWORDS

Search engine marketing, also known as Pay Per Click advertising, can be a great source of membership leads. For the uninitiated it can seem overwhelming, but it's actually a pretty simple concept. As people search for keywords in their search engine, results are loaded. Most results shown are called "organic" results. These are websites who the search engine has deemed or "ranked" as the most relevant to the topic that was searched. There are other results which have paid to be displayed alongside the organic ones. Those are the pay-per-click ads.

Pay-per-click ads, or PPC for short, is based off a bidding system. If there are two or more organizations who are paying for that keyword or phrase, the one who bids higher has a better chance of getting the prime spot up at the top of the organic results. I say "better chance" because paying more is not necessarily a guarantee. There are other factors in play.

Another important element is relevance, which is gauged by how many people click on the ad when it's displayed. Let's say there are two ads which are served to 100 people each. If ten people click on an ad "A" with a $1 bid that's better than if three people clicked on ad "B" that has a $2 bid. The search engine is going to make $10 off ad "A", and only $6 off ad "B". They'll deem ad "A" to be more compelling and thus serve that ad to more people. That's why it's important to not just bid high, but to carefully choose what keywords and phrases you'd like to bid for and craft a compelling ad that is consistent with those search terms.

Far and away, Google is the leader in paid search. Paid search accounts for the vast majority of Google's revenue and as such they place a lot of emphasis on it. There are two forms of Google ad revenue, standard PPC ads and retargeting. Standard ads are displayed in Google's search engine and are text only and can't contain images. Google ads can also be served on sites across the web that participate in Google's network, which they call the "display network". These may be retailers, online publications and blogs, review sites and a host of other pages across the web. Display network ads can be either graphic-based or text-only. It depends on what the particular network partner decides.

Retargeting happens only on the display network. This is when an ad from a particular website is served to someone who has visited a site in the past. If you've ever been on Facebook or another random website and you have seen an ad for those shoes you were shopping for last week from another site, you've been retargeted.

Retargeting works by installing a tracker called a "cookie" on your computer when you're browsing. That cookie is attached to your machine and it is a unique identifier Google uses to follow your actions across the web. This scares some people, but you should know that the data is hashed, which means personal information has been stripped away. Cookies do not store data on who you are, they only keep a history of actions that you took. That may or may not comfort folks when it comes to their privacy concerns, but it's a reality in our world today. As a marketer, this information is invaluable because it help builds a profile for a prospect.

Volumes have been written on the subject of PPC strategy, so I'm not going to bore you here with the ins and outs of it. There are, however, a few tips that I think will serve you well if you venture into this world.

KEYWORD TIPS

Long tail keywords, which are specific phrases, will give you your best shot at maximizing your PPC budget because less people will be bidding for them and the users will be much more targeted. "Golf" is a broad keyword. "Golf in Tampa" is a little better but still pretty broad. "Best Country Club in South Tampa" is a long tail keyword and is a much more specific search. You're not just targeting golfers, you're now targeting someone who's looking for a private club. You're also narrowing it by vicinity or neighborhood. You're also using a word that people commonly search, the word "best". This is much more granular and your CPC will decrease.

Google's Keyword tool is a great free resource to find out which phrases are commonly being searched. Once you find a few, put them into Google AdWords and the system will give you an approximation of what you'll need to bid in order for your ad to get served. Look for some long tail keywords that people aren't bidding for and you'll have an economical way to send more traffic to your site and more prospects that call to schedule a tour.

Excluding certain keywords is just as important as finding the right ones. Google AdWords makes it easy to tell it what searches you don't want to be associated with. You might want to exclude the search term of simply "golf club" because you'll mix in with people who are actually searching for equipment rather than places. Take a look at what search terms are being used and make sure they are relevant to what your ad is speaking to. You might be surprised at what comes up.

WRITING PPC AD COPY

Your ad copy should include the exact keywords and phrases that you're bidding for. If the keyword phrase you are targeting is "country club in Tampa", then your ad should read something like "The most exclusive country club in Tampa. Register for your VIP tour." In that ad, I'm using the exact phrase and it's going to do better because users will recognize that it's extremely relevant to what they typed.

Because your character count is limited on Google AdWords and other systems, you'll want to be straightforward and to the point. You really can't do too much teasing. People are savvy and want to know what they're getting into before they proceed. You have to tell people what they're going to get and make it compelling enough they'll want to click.

You should use as many characters as you're allowed. You want your ad to take up the most amount of real estate the platform will allow. That's going to give you your best chance of catching attention and therefore success. Don't add fluffy words just to fill the space though. Make sure it's relevant to your offer.

LANDING PAGES AND A/B TESTING

The end result of any online ad, PPC or otherwise, that drives traffic to your site is to get someone to take the next action. This doesn't mean browsing your site. In fact, you should never send someone who clicks on your ad to your home page. That's a gigantic waste of your ad budget. You should always drive traffic to a page which has a specific offer directly associated to the search term they used and to the ad copy you wrote. When I say action, I mean filling out a form, picking up the phone, or sending you an email. It's much harder to get people to write in or email so your best bet is to capture their contact info.

You'll want to limit what you ask for in a form however. The longer the form and the more details you request, the less likely people will fill it out. I suggest clubs ask for name, email and a phone number. That's it. Don't ask questions like interests, hobbies, occupation, net worth, mailing address or any of that. Just capture the basics.

Now getting people to fill out that form is a whole different ballgame. You need to have a very compelling offer. Please don't get me wrong, I'm not suggesting a discount or coupon or anything of the sort. Those things only serve to devalue your brand and your image. A compelling offer might be a PDF guide to playing better golf, or it might be an eBook or a newsletter filled with useful tips. It could also be things like a preview round of golf or a VIP cocktail reception or open house. Those types of things will generate leads for a landing page.

One particular landing page we built recently that generated a lot of good leads was a raffle form where folks could have a chance to win a foursome at a Naples, Florida golf club. They were served information about becoming a member alongside a chance to preview the club with their friends. People filled it out in droves and it was a big differentiator in a crowded market filled with golf clubs. It also gave a lot of exposure to a club that had once been considered "a hidden gem".

You'll want to continually tweak your landing pages to see what converts into action and what doesn't. You should also split test whenever possible. You can send half the traffic from your PPC ad to one page and the other half to another with some different graphics, headlines and offers. See which one works and then send more traffic to the winner next month while also trying something new out. Keep repeating this until you have the conversion numbers you need.

ANCHOR CONTENT

Assuming you now have built some traffic to your site you need to capitalize on it. It's not enough to get people there, you've got to turn those visitors into leads. As I've mentioned, it takes something compelling to get people to give you their information. No one is just going to hand over their email address. That's where what I call anchor content comes in.

Anchor content is one irresistible piece of content that you can offer a visitor to your site in exchange for their info. On my sites, I generally use an eBook to accomplish this goal. If you want to learn the *7 Elements of Highly Effective Ads*, simply enter your name and email and I'll send you my 47-page book. On another site, one devoted to my private club consulting practice, I have the *The Top 25 Traits of Great Private Clubs*. Lots of people download these books and it helps me build my list.

Now, the books are in fact good. They are filled with valuable info and some of my best ideas and insights. If they weren't, it would undermine my entire value proposition and I would have an angry visitor on my hands. You don't want to let people down because you'll not only lose your chances with a potential member, they'll often tell other people to stay away. The goal to shoot for is to always deliver ten times the value that people expect. If you do that, you'll build a list that is dying to open your emails when they arrive in their inbox.

Anchor content doesn't have to be eBooks. It could be audio, video, a guide or some other interactive resource. Just make sure it's valuable to the visitor.

EMAIL CAMPAIGNS

If you spend any time following the major marketing gurus out there, they will tell you that the most valuable asset to develop as a marketer is a healthy email list. Email is simply the most effective long-term digital strategy there is. It just works. Since this book is about building your membership, I'm not going to cover emailing your members in this section. We're going to focus on creating and nurturing a list of prospects.

LIST BUILDING

Email lists can be purchased just like snail mail lists. You can specify age, gender, income, and all of the other interests that you can specify with postal data. However, for the most part I've never had a ton of success with lists that were purchased. They are usually extremely cold and I believe they are often people's throw away email. You know, that extra address folks keep to send all the spam to? You probably have one of those. I certainly do.

When you're emailing an ice cold list like this you're basically spamming. Even if someone has "opted in" which is email marketing lingo for allowed their email to be used for marketing purposes (i.e., shared with partners and outside vendors), they've probably done so unwittingly or accidentally. Websites make it so easy to miss unchecking the opt-in box or they stealthily bury it someplace you're not expecting to find it. Some altogether ignore your request to opt out. At any rate, these lists rarely work and I council clubs to avoid them.

127

What does work, however, is building a natural list of actual interested prospects from your website and from your social media connections. We just covered anchor content and that's the easiest way to accomplish this. However there is a host of other ways.

I recently came across an ingenious way to capture folks email addresses who are interested in membership. BallenIsles Country Club in South Florida requires that web visitors enter a valid email address in order to download their membership brochure. How perfect! This weeds out people who are just browsing around and gets warm leads flowing for those who are truly interested in membership. Their whole site is great from a content perspective and one that I would encourage other clubs to model.

There are offline methods too. If your club sets up at trade shows and conventions, like boat shows for instance, you can offer some sort of raffle prize in exchange for email addresses. If you do a lot of networking, you can build your list from the folks you meet at local events. I would suggest you ask them before you just pop them on your list though. Nobody appreciates being added without their permission. However, you should make sure to ask so it sounds like you're doing *them* a favor. After you've developed some rapport with the person you could say something like, "Hey, would you like me to put you on our mailing list? We send our newsletter out once a month and it's filled with golf tips, recipes and other goodies. I think you'd get a lot out of it." Who's going to say no to something like that?

Lastly, you should be collecting emails and phone numbers from every guest who walks through your door.

Once again, you want there to be a perceived benefit to the person and not just make it a chore. Tell them what they'll get out of signing up or offer them a small perk for doing so. If you have some sort of mobile application, like a course guide with GPS yardage for instance, make sure it sits behind a signup page where users are required to enter their info. If you wanted to do that same thing but in an analog way, you could offer yardage books to players who give you their contact info. I think you'll find most would be more than willing to exchange their email for a perk they found valuable like that.

FREQUENCY & CONTENT

The first question I'm usually asked is, "How often should I email my prospects?" My answer is not less than once per month and not more than one per week. The most important thing about emailing prospects is that you constantly deliver value. The minute you forsake that strategy, and simply ask for a sale and nothing more, you'll get a quick unsubscribe. Your job as an email marketer is to provide useful, relevant and timely information. If this sounds a lot like that blog I suggested you create, you're right. In fact, you can repurpose the content here to make your life a little easier.

After sending thousands and thousands of emails, there's a strategy that I've honed that seems to work best. Every email I send, or coach my clients to craft, has three parts. The first is the value add. The second is the update. The third is the call to action. I'll break down each of them for you.

129

THE VALUE ADD

The first question everyone wants answered when they open your email will be, "So what's in it for me?" As such, it's vital you address this immediately or risk losing their attention. What it is can and should change with each eblast. We discussed earlier in Membership is Not a Sprint, how a variable reward system is crucial to habit formation. So whether it's advice, a tip, a top 5 list, or some irresistible offer, make sure you put that right up front in your email blast and change it up from month to month.

THE UPDATE

The update section is next and it's nothing more than news and updates that would be relevant to the reader. The reason I include this section in my emails is because I've found that people love hearing about developments. Progress is exciting. No one wants the same old same old. They want to see continual evolution and innovation. That signals to them that you're special and forward thinking. Everything else they buy improves, from their homes to their tech to their automobiles, so why shouldn't their experience?

Some things you can update folks on include facilities that you're building, new items that are being added to your menus, new classes or groups that are forming, new renovations, new equipment and more. And by the way, if you're sitting there reading this and you have nothing new going on at your club I'd recommend you fix that first. Stagnation is a very good predictor of membership decline.

THE CALL TO ACTION

Don't ever send an email without providing one, and only one, clear call to action (CTA). Your CTA needs to be singular and it needs to be direct. That means, you shouldn't have multiple links to different places, a phone number to call, and an email address to write to. You should pick one option.

Also, don't be vague. Don't say things like "Give us a call today" or "Check out our website". Instead you should have a big button that says things like "Click here to schedule your tour" or "Book a complimentary lesson with our pro today" or "Join us for a VIP cocktail reception". These are much more powerful.

Just like I touched on in the pay per click section, you'll want traffic coming from your emails to direct to a specific page on your site, never the home page or a generic page. Make sure the page is not cluttered or filled with fluff. Place only the essentials and the form in as clear a fashion as possible. If they took the time to click on your eblast they are ready to go. Don't give them any distractions that would let them back out.

AUTOMATION & AUTORESPONDERS

If you're this far into the book, you certainly know that your plate is full of tasks that you should be accomplishing. I highly recommend that you put your emails on autopilot and avoid the stress and hassle of manually sending and keeping track of new subscribers. This can be accomplished by setting up an autoresponder series within your email program. If your email program does not have this feature, this would be a good time to make the switch. I use MailChimp as my mass email blast system. In addition to being extremely intuitive and fun, they have dynamite automation tools. If you're looking for a new system, give them a try. I prefer it over Constant Contact and some of the others out there.

A good autoresponder system will allow you to set up a series of emails that will be sent to the user at particular intervals. For instance, you might send a welcome immediately after they sign up. After that, you might set the system to send emails every two weeks for a period of twelve weeks. Each of those emails will have some new content that you've created. Hopefully you'll use the system similar to what I described above by including a value add, an update and a call to action. After that the autoresponder series ends and they'll simply be emailed when you send out your mass communications to the list.

What I described above will work for 80% of the clubs out there. But if you want to go deeper and refine this even more, you can drill these automated emails down further by specifying what email is sent to the user depending on a previous action that they took. This is sometimes referred to as a "trigger".

Here's an example of how a trigger works. Email #1 is sent out. If the user clicks, they'll be served email #2 version A. If they do not click, they'll be served email #2 version B. This process can repeat infinitely. You can define triggers like opening the email, clicking on a link and more, depending on your email provider. This will take some time to develop, but once you've got a system like this, you'll be freed up to do some of those other important tasks on our list.

MOBILE APPS

Mobile applications for smartphones and tablets are a great way to serve and delight the existing membership. Just by the sheer fact that your club has an app, you're signaling to the public that your club is evolving and cares about improving the experience. However, mobile apps can also be used in a powerful way as a marketing engine for the club. They do this by capturing guest information and then providing useful tools that guests want to use. This opens up the opportunity to request some personal data.

There are features I think your app should have that would make it attractive for guests. Things like GPS, live weather, a food and beverage ordering system and a scoring system would make a day or a round at your club much more enjoyable. In order to access those features, people need to be willing to download it to their device, sign up and provide their information. I've actually created a couple of these apps for clubs, and from experience I can tell you it works.

The great thing about an app is once someone has downloaded it, you're literally in their pocket and can market to them whenever you wish. You can send them push notifications, and messages right through the app. Of course, the same rules apply here as they do to email blasts and other forms of marketing—you need to deliver value first and sell second. You also don't want to message them too often. If you can maintain the right balance though, you'll have a direct channel into their world for as long as they keep the app on their phone. I would suggest sending no more than one message per week to prospects via a push notification.

If you're worried about privacy, you'll be ok too. With these apps you can keep member specific information behind a password protected area of the app, or grant access to those sections only to members by asking them to enter a member identification number when they first sign up.

PUBLIC RELATIONS

There's an alternative way to soft market your club that has no outlay, save for time. It's called public relations and it's one of the most often overlooked strategies. In order to do PR right, you don't need to hire a PR firm. You just need to learn how to tell a good story and be able to pitch it.

PRESS RELEASES

Should you use the press release in your marketing strategy? The short answer is yes, but with a caveat. Press releases aren't used like they once were. Back in the day, you would draft a release and send it to all the local news agencies in town, places like newspapers, television and radio stations. If it was a story worth telling they would pick it up and contact you to set up an interview. Today it's a good strategy for online publications and blogs, but doesn't work so well for the larger news organizations.

When writing a release be sure to follow a standard format. Templates can be found online easily. You need your contact details up at the top, a captivating headline and few paragraphs that explain the who, what, when, where and why. Often, news agencies copy verbatim from the release so be sure to write it in a newspaper article style, giving the most important details up front and expounding further down the page. If you're uncomfortable writing these, they are fairly inexpensive to outsource.

PITCHING YOUR STORY

While press releases can still work occasionally, I've found you'll have better luck reaching out directly to a reporter or producer by phone or via email. Most media outlets list their key people's contact information right on the website. Otherwise a quick Google search can usually do the trick. Also, don't forget that most journalists are on Twitter or Instagram or some other social network. I've heard a lot of success stories from folks who send them private messages through social platforms, especially video messages. It works because it's different and stands out. You've probably figured out by now that extraordinary always wins.

When pitching a story you need to think about your local morning news show. What are the types of things they cover? Some ideas include:

- Seasonal Recipes from your chef (news agencies love seasonal content)

- Food and Wine Pairings from your F&B director

- Community outreach projects and other charitable contributions from the club

- Summer Gardening tips from your director of agronomy

- Shedding the extra holiday pounds from your fitness director

Getting featured on television is as simple as figuring out a trending topic and getting creative. Watch some news shows and figure out what they like to report on. Find an angle that's out of the ordinary or has some built-in shock or wow factor. That will give you your best shot at standing out from the other news stories that are pitched.

CONTESTS AND AWARDS

The general public thinks that awards and designations happen purely by chance. The seasoned marketer knows that they are a PR strategy, often lobbied or paid for. I recommend all my club clients enter as many local, national and international awards as they can. I think it should be a line item in the marketing budget. They bring prestige to the club in the eyes of the public and pride to the eyes of the member and staff.

The F&B Department of your club is an easy place to start. Get your chef recognized as one of the top culinary experts in your community. Whether it's a blue ribbon at the town's chili cook-off or a James Beard Award, make them a star. Once you do, get them featured in the news. It's an easy pitch.

There are national and regional publications that love to create lists of all shapes and sizes. Best golf courses, best communities, best places to work, best cuisine, the list goes on. Apply to every one of these that you can and put them on display in a conspicuous location for members, guest and staff to admire.

BONUS PR HACK: ANSWERING QUERIES

Did you know there are hundreds of reporters right now seeking a source to quote or contribute to their news story? Some people get nervous when they think of contacting a reporter but the reality is, they need you. The news moves fast, and deadlines are tight in that business. That means they need to find someone quickly to give them a take they can use.

One service that I recommend you sign up for is called Help a Reporter Out, or HARO for short. Each day, three times a day, journalists both locally and nationally send in their stories and request replies back from experts. An email goes out to all the users who have claimed to be an expert in a given field and they are given selected stories to comment on when applicable. There could be stories related to business development, networking, athletics, fitness, wellness, food and beverage and more that you and your staff are uniquely qualified to answer. Best of all, this service is 100% free to use.

This is exactly the strategy that I've personally used to get featured in Entrepreneur® and many other sites across the web. I answered a HARO query with a unique perspective and the reporter ran with it. Two things that will make you successful on HARO are responding promptly to queries (often within the first 15 minutes of the email arriving) and having an outside-the-box perspective to offer. The standard fare just won't cut it most of the time.

In addition to HARO there are other services that work in a similar fashion. It's a fun way to get exposure, build your credibility and get some powerful links coming back to your site.

These are many of the different tactics and strategies you can use to expand your reach, increase visibility and raise brand awareness. In today's fast, digital world, the options are continually expanding, but the basic principles remain the same—find out where your audience is, appeal to their emotions and engage them on a regular basis. In the next chapter, you'll learn how to make your advertising work more effectively.

NOTES:

7

CHAPTER SEVEN

CREATING EFFECTIVE ADS

THE 6 TYPES OF ADS

O k, so now that we have our marketing channels down, it's time to focus on effective communication strategies. In this section I'm going to show you a blueprint for crafting the perfect ad. I'm also going to teach you about the membership marketing lifecycle and how you should adjust your message for each stage of the journey.

There's a common misconception out there that an ad is an ad is an ad. In reality, there are different types of ads that can be effectively used at certain times of a customer or, in our case, member's lifecycle. Some ads do hard selling, and some ads do not even sell at all. I generally break ads into 6 unique types: Intrigue Building, Emotion Setting, Social Proof, Immediate Purchase Drivers, Feature Focused and The Reminder.

You've heard the term, "timing is everything," and it's absolutely a fact in marketing and advertising. Serving the right type of ad at the right time is the first key to success. So it follows that understanding the membership lifecycle is a key component to crafting effective advertisements. Every future club member will progress through the following lifecycle phases in this order: Unaware Prospect, Aware Prospect, Interested Prospect, New Member, Tenured Member, and finally Past Member.

Before we move on, I should make it clear that the inverse is true. Serving the wrong type of ad at the wrong time can yield poor results. But all too many times, I see management and membership folks who are unaware a difference exists.

I'm going to break down each type of ad. I will show you the pros and cons to each type. I'll also discuss the best time in the member's lifecycle to use each type. I'm confident that if you follow these guidelines, you're going to have a much higher chance of success in your marketing efforts.

INTRIGUE BUILDING ADS

Intrigue building ads might just be the most fun. These ads try to capture your attention or pique your interest. They are generally minimalist and always vague. Oftentimes they are cryptic, being only a web address or an icon for instance. If you've ever driven down the highway and seen a billboard displaying only a web address and nothing else, you've seen an Intrigue Building Ad. Recently I was driving down the road in Tampa and saw an ad for the social network Snapchat that was only the little ghost icon of the company and nothing more. That piqued my interest, as I'm sure it did the other drivers, whether they recognized the icon or not.

When my consulting partnership, ClubMark Partners, made our announcement that we would be displaying at the CMAA World Conference & Expo, we sent an email to managers that was cryptic. Since no one knew who we were, we decided to have a little fun with it. The conference was in Florida so we used a picture of a huge footprint on the beach, something big-foot size. The email read, "Something BIG is coming!" We listed the booth number and invited people to come. That was it. We didn't even include the full logo, just the symbol so that they would recognize it when they came to our booth. It was fun and suspenseful and that's what these types of ads are all about.

PROS

These ads are very easy to remember or recall. In the case of that cryptic web address billboard, a potential member only needs to remember the website. The call to action and the message of the ad are one in the same.

Another positive is that they are generally simple and uncluttered. The message is front and center and impossible to get lost. The best ads, no matter the type, are the ones that communicate clearly without clutter.

These ads get people talking and that's always a good thing. This is water cooler fodder at its best. Any advertiser would love to hear a couple of people standing around saying, "Hey, did you see that billboard on I-95? What the heck was that?"

CONS

The most obvious drawback of the Intrigue Building Ad is there is a longer time from sight to sale. This means there must be a higher level of dedication on the part of the advertiser because they are likely not going to get a return on investment immediately. This is a long-term strategy and it's definitely not for everybody or clubs with limited budgets.

The second negative to this type of ad is the potential for the message to be ignored or forgotten. It's very much an "all or nothing" approach in that way. If the web address, image or message isn't memorable, that's a whole lot of wasted resources.

TIMING

This ad is best used on the Unaware Prospect. If done right, it begins to turn them into an Aware Prospect. In some cases it can be effectively used for a Tenured Member or Past Member, but it's rare to see.

EMOTION SETTING ADS

Emotion setting ads are a personal favorite of mine. These types of ads create a feeling or an emotion in a prospective or existing member's mind. It plants a subtle psychological seed. Most often, you'll see this type of ad used in the luxury space. The best example I can give would be a women's fashion brand like Chanel or Coach. Often, you'll see ads for these brands in women's magazines where a model is pictured in a scene with the product strategically placed within the vignette. Usually the brand's logo will be in a corner or off to the side, sometimes accompanied by a short positioning statement. Something like, "Modern luxury redefined," or "An experience like no other."

Remember, the more expensive the product or service the more that selling to the emotional side of the brain is necessary. Rolex, Cartier, Coach, Louis Vuitton, Mercedes Benz and other fine products and services take this approach and do it very well. They understand that their clients are savvy and less susceptible to standard marketing messages and tactics. Instead, they offer something less obvious that leaves people wanting more. It's addition by subtraction.

PROS

Looking at ads like these, it's nearly impossible not to have an emotional reaction or response. That's a good thing, as we've discussed. Purchasing decisions happen in the emotional brain.

These ads associate desire with the brand. That's never a bad thing.

CONS

It's difficult for these ads to have impact unless there is already some level of brand recognition. This type of ad will absolutely not work for you if no one has heard of you prior to coming across it.

TIMING

This type of ad should be served to Aware Prospects, Current Members or Past Members.

SOCIAL PROOF ADS

Social Proof is a powerful type of ad that taps into a primal motivator inside of human beings. It's an inherent human desire to want to be accepted and part of a homogenous group. Social Proof ads use happy members to do the selling, thus tapping into that human need. They are often testimonials from peers. These types of ads rely on stats, before and after motifs, and quotes from happy members.

If you've ever come across an infomercial for a piece of exercise equipment or an ad in a magazine for a weight loss supplement and seen a before and after photo of a happy customer who has shed hundreds of pounds, you've been advertised to through Social Proof. They are using results from other happy customers to turn you into one.

Another great example of a Social Proof ad is the old McDonald's hamburger ticker. On the signpost of every McDonald's around the world, they proclaimed the on-going count of burgers they had served to hungry customers. "Over 85 million served," turned into "Billions and Billions Served," in under 50 years. It was a powerful way for McDonald's to show their brand dominance, as well as convince other hungry folks that a lot of others in the neighborhood enjoyed a meal there, too.

I always recommend to my clients that they gather up social proof from their members and begin to share these stories frequently. Whether it's written down or recorded to video, these messages can be used strategically for the club's marketing efforts.

PROS

The first positive of the Social Proof ad is that it sneaks in the back door. It often gets past the initial barrier that we all put up to some degree of not wanting to be sold to. In general, folks in western culture are wary of the salesperson. Social Proof uses others in our relative socio-economic strata to do the selling for them. In that way they slip past our defenses.

They also tap into the human instinct to form a tribe. We all want to be part of something bigger than ourselves. If others are doing it, we want to join in. It's natural, and that's why these ads work.

CONS

These ads are reliant on the subject matter connecting and resonating with the target audience. If they don't, they are useless. We can use the previous example of a hot new diet supplement that helps folks lose hundreds of pounds. If that ad is served to a person who is in shape and at or below their target weight, it falls on deaf ears.

TIMING

Social Proof ads work best for Interested Prospects. They usually give the last push towards the sale. Secondarily, they can also be used for Unaware Prospects to get them to become Aware. This type of ad is not as powerful when directed at Past Members or Tenured Members.

IMMEDIATE PURCHASE DRIVER

The immediate purchase driver is an ad that asks for the sale and makes no bones about it. Fast food chains advertising a $4.99 value meal is a classic example. These ads display the price front and center and hope that you're craving what they have to offer. In fact, they rely heavily on timing. Retail products, especially on the lower end of the market, often employ this tactic as well.

Ikea is a master at this ad type. They show off their Nordic inspired furnishings on stark, colorless backgrounds and slap a price and a logo right on the ad. They work when the right combo of price and desire meet in the consumer's gaze.

PROS

These ads generate immediate membership sales. Who doesn't want that?

CONS

Your offer has to be priced *and* timed right, which is difficult in many cases.

Often these ads are discount or deal driven. Discounts devalue your brand. Anytime you discount something, it sets a lower bar of expectation in a consumer's mind and makes it harder for you to sell at full price later in the lifecycle. It also disenfranchises members who have paid full price when they joined.

TIMING

Inherently, this type of ad is delivered just before the sale or the Interested Prospect Phase.

These ads can also work very well for Current Members and Tenured Members. Telling a member there is a $25++ fee to attend the Easter Brunch is necessary to drive reservations.

FEATURE & BENEFIT FOCUSED ADS

This ad is the most common and it's also the weakest in my opinion. In fact, the Feature & Benefit Ad is pretty much the impetus for me writing this section of the book. Throughout the years I've seen more clubs employ this type of ad with little to no success. The reason this type of ad rarely works well is because it's completely reliant on the logical side of the brain—that same part that resists being sold to. To be fair, there are certain personalities that this ad type appeals to. But in my experience, those are the hardest and most demanding types of members you'll ever have.

149

These ads often list bullet points of features and benefits. They're also very long-winded in comparison to the other ad types. Why is that? Well, of course there's so much to say about how amazing this product or service is in comparison to the competition!

All kidding aside, I only recommend this ad type in small doses and when it's working in conjunction with the other ad types mentioned.

PROS

The benefit of this ad is that it appeals to folks out there who have analytical minds. If you want to reach that segment of the population, this ad type will do it for you.

Because so much information is included in this ad type, it potentially makes it easier for the consumer to have all the facts in once place.

CONS

These ads are often busy and cluttered visually or verbally, depending on the medium used. When consumers have a hard time focusing, they have a hard time buying.

As mentioned before, logic is not a strong motivator in the buying process. Because purchases happen in the emotional side of the brain, this can actually become a hinderance.

TIMING

As you can probably tell, I don't recommend these ads during the prospect phases. While it's important to have this logic oriented info on your website when people ask, it shouldn't be front and center in your marketing materials.

These ads can be used effectively during the Past Member, Member, or Tenured Member phase, however. Remember, emotional purchases are justified by logical reasoning. This ad could prevent buyer's remorse. And in the case of member events like the Easter brunch, people often want to know exactly what will be on the menu or agenda.

REMINDER AD

This type of ad follows up with current or former members of your club. This ad can be used as an upsell or introduction of a new product or service. It can also be used to reach out to resignees.

You'll often see these types of ads in email form. A company that does it great is Trip Advisor. I once left a review for a new hotel that was very popular with readers and every few weeks they'll remind me to come back and leave another review because my other performed so well. They weren't pushy. Instead they stroked my ego, and the constant reaching back eventually drove me to action.

PROS

As we've discussed before, the easiest person to sell is the one you've already sold to, so you're more likely to have better conversions. If done right, presenting improved or new product and service lines shows members you're investing in their experience and this increases customer loyalty dramatically.

CONS

This type of ad only works well if there is a laser target focus to Tenured Members or Past Members. Be careful not to inundate them with too many marketing messages or you risk losing them and getting unsubscribed from.

TIMING

Naturally, this ad only works in the Tenured Member and Past Member phases.

7 STEP ADVERTISING BLUEPRINT

Now that we have set goals and put practices in place to measure our results as well as done a split test and/or used a focus group, it's time to get down to crafting the perfect ad. Below is my seven step system that you can implement today to start creating more effective ads. No matter the medium, and no matter where your customer is in their lifecycle, this system will get your ads more engagement and will generate more leads when followed in the order I've laid out for you.

STEP 1. START WITH THE ENDGAME IN MIND

The first thing to decide on with any ad is the action you would like the reader or listener to take. In marketing terminology, this is called the "call to action" or CTA. Often, I find folks don't put nearly enough emphasis on the CTA. They think of it, but only as an afterthought. Since it's the single way you'll actually generate sales from ads, I think it should be at the forefront of the entire ad creation process. The best CTA's have four things in common. They are singular, direct, simple and are the focal point of the ad.

SINGULAR

Your CTA should be one action, and one action only. Whether that's picking up the phone and calling you, navigating to your website, downloading your app or something else, there should be one simple action you want your target prospect to make.

Very often, clients ask me and my team to create ads that have a phone, fax, website, physical address, social media profiles and every other form of contact under the sun all on one page. They want to make sure all of their bases are covered. The problem is, it confuses the message and when you give people too many options, they often choose nothing.

Think about it, if potential members want to find you on Facebook, they'll look for you. There's no need to have the bright blue Facebook icon take up valuable space or distract your audience from simply picking up the phone and calling you or typing in your web address.

So find the one action you want people to take and make that the only thing you put on your ad. I know it's going to be tough to pick just one, but you can do it. And if you trust me, you're going to have a lot better results.

DIRECT

I strongly recommend using direct lines of communication in your call to action. What do I mean by that? Instead of taking someone to your home page, have them browse or click to a specific landing page related to the publication or medium they found you on (i.e. - privateclubradio.com/webinar). On that page you might have a specific offer for folks who found you that way. Finding ways to personalize the experience is something I stress in today's impersonal world.

If your CTA is a phone number, don't just have them call the main line and get a receptionist. Give them a direct number or a direct extension to someone who can discuss the offer right away.

If your CTA is asking someone to email you, have them email something that is related to the publication or advertising medium they found you on (i.e., ebook@privateclubagency.com). It's subtle, but it will strike a psycho-logical chord and people will be more likely to remember it.

The fewer hoops you make your prospects jump through, the more likely you are to get a purchase decision.

SIMPLE

If using a website, make it as short and direct as possible. Don't make people type in a bunch of dashes, symbols or forward slashes. Same goes for an email address, make it one easy-to-remember word, not a phrase.

THE FOCAL POINT

So often, I see CTA's that are just squeezed in at the bottom. Why is that? Do businesses not want people to find them? I suggest using color and boldness to draw the eye to the CTA. Make it the brightest thing on the page or screen. Use visual clues and balance to draw the eye to the CTA. You'll get a lot more calls or clicks, I promise.

STEP 2. CREATE WITH YOUR TARGET IN MIND

Design the words and look of the ad with your target in mind. Every club should have a clear picture of who their avatar is. Avatar is marketing terminology for your perfect prospect and the embodiment of your average member. Find out as much as you can about your avatar. How old they are, how much money they make, if they're a certain race, gender or ethnic group, where they live, what they like and dislike and more. Be as detailed as you possibly can when you create your avatar.

Look at your current membership base and see if you can build a typical profile from there. Often if you go through your member list, some patterns will start to emerge. You might even be surprised at what you find.

If you're a newer club, you're going to have to take an educated guess or conduct a focus group to find out who your target is. But even if you're slightly off, I promise your ad will do better than the one from a club who just tries to advertise broadly to everybody.

STEP 3. DESIGN FOR THE MEDIUM THAT WILL BE USED

Think about where your ad or campaign will be placed before you make it. Ads and marketing are not a panacea. You can't just make a single version of an ad, splash it all over the place and expect to get results. The best ads are tailored to a specific audience and designed around the medium in which they are going to be used and the place they will be seen.

It's highly likely that you'll need to change the copy or swap graphics and photos depending on the demographics of the publication you're placing it in. Brands who are successful do this all the time. BMW ads in an auto aficionado magazine like *Car and Driver* might highlight technical specs, while the ads they place in a men's style magazine like *GQ* might show off the car's sleek curves and stylish design. It's a different audience, so they speak to them in a different way. If your club has both golf and tennis you wouldn't want to put the same ad in *Golf Week* as you do in *Inside Tennis*, for instance.

Technical things may change, too. The color balance of an ad placed in a glossy magazine will look far different than the same ad placed on newsprint. Also, the images will print differently and micro details may get lost. Have your designer adjust accordingly.

STEP 4. CHOOSE YOUR WORDS CAREFULLY

There are words that mean roughly the same thing, but the psychological impact or associations can be very different. For instance, I never use the word "cheap", I always say, "inexpensive". "Cheap" suggests qualities like flimsy, shoddy, and generally sub-par. Inexpensive, on the other hand, simply costs less, but does not imply a lack of value. The word "affordable" means something different all together.

When someone is going to spend their marketing money with me there is not a "cost", they are making an "investment". The implication being that there will be a return on that investment and they are not just blindly throwing their money at me. A "cost" is a pain point, but an "investment" is a means to a future pleasure. My agency provides design and marketing "services" not "work". Who wants more work? Not me, but I'd certainly appreciate some service!

Stay away from cliché phrases at all cost. Trite phrases like "the best kept secret" or "taking you to the next level" are cringe-worthy and often really not the impression you want to give. Doesn't "best kept secret" really mean no one's ever heard of you?

So think about the words you choose wisely, and you will go a long way to winning more business. Also, consider hiring a copywriter or an agency with copywriting capabilities if you need help.

STEP 5. CREATE AN EFFECTIVE HEADLINE

I would argue the headline is the most important piece of visual information on the ad. As such, it deserves the most care and attention.

In print ads and collateral, keep headlines to a seven word maximum. Just like billboards, headlines should be short, sweet and to the point. Flowery language and copy that is full of adjectives doesn't do the job. Think of your headline like a billboard that will capture people as they go through life at 80 miles an hour.

STEP 6. CRAFT SHORT, EMOTIONALLY-FOCUSED AD COPY

Most ad copy should be no more than one or two paragraphs. If we're talking about print, one is the maximum. Force yourself to edit. Just like I mentioned above, people are moving fast. I know it's hard, but keeping it to one paragraph will help you pitch your product or service with focus and clarity.

Attention spans are getting shorter. An ad isn't the medium to explain everything there is to know about your product or service. An ad is designed to get someone's attention and move them along the path of your customer lifecycle.

As I've mentioned before, people buy for emotional reasons. So make sure your words are written in a way that appeals to that side of the brain. Focus on what someone will gain personally instead of a bulleted list of features and benefits.

STEP 7. CHOOSE COLORS & DESIGN THE IMAGERY

The last step in our process is generally where poor performing ads start. But just because it's last in my process, doesn't mean it's not vitally important. You should carefully consider the colors and imagery of your ad.

First and foremost, the colors you use should be true to your club's brand. Imagery should be consistent to the look of your brand. Fonts or typefaces should match what you have on signage, collateral pieces and your website.

Great brands know consistency is crucial. Most strong brands have a style guide that shows the fonts, colors, and graphic elements that should be maintained. They understand how vital consistent imagery and style can be. Just think about the Coca-Cola red. You can see that red and think of Coke almost immediately. In fact, in 2015 they released cans that didn't even have their name on them. It was just their red and their swoop, and they still sold well. Incredible! Now, you may never have the brand recognition Coca-Cola does, but your icon, colors, and font type can certainly become a memorable element to your target audience or avatar.

Visual consistency is often taken for granted or an afterthought, but it shouldn't be. I spoke about this earlier in the book but it's worth reinforcing here once again. Consistency is the foundation upon which the sales process is built. Consistency leads to an expectation in the mind of the customer. And once an expectation is continually met, customers develop a trust. When trust is reinforced, it leads to sales.

The inverse is also true and can have dire consequences. A lack of consistency leads to no expectations, distrust and lost customers. Worse yet, those unhappy customers usually tell their friends. That is the reverse of your goal.

Another tip I'd like to share with you is that people are attracted to people. Find ways to get faces of people in your imagery when it's appropriate and you'll have a better chance of success. There's just something innate in all of us that is drawn to people. It's similar to our earlier discussion on social proof. Faces are a form of social proof. Instead of just a landscape shot of your golf course or interior shot of your club's restaurant, have a designer Photoshop some people into the scene. You'll get much better results.

The last thing I want to mention is to never accept a free design from an ad salesperson. Newspapers, magazines and other media outlets often offer design services as a value-added benefit. While it may seem like you're making a smart financial decision in the short term, the consequences to your branding and consistency will outweigh the savings. The good folks doing that design work are generally not paid well and consequently the ad suffers due to a lack of care and consideration. Even the good ones don't have a vested interest in your club's brand, and aren't familiar with your unique story. If you don't have someone on your staff who is capable of designing or creating your ads, hire a designer or agency that has experience in your industry. The few bucks you pay them will go miles in terms of quality, impact and overall consistency with your brand. There's a quote I've seen attributed to Benjamin Franklin that I love. "The bitterness of poor quality remains long after the sweetness of lower price is forgotten."

So now you have the tools to create an effective ad. Make sure to follow the steps in order. Your ads will be more effective and they'll lead to more membership leads if you do.

NOTES:

8

CHAPTER EIGHT

VISION OF THE FUTURE

Should you be looking forward to what's coming down the road or should you be concerned? In this last section of the book I'm going to lay out for you where I see our industry headed. Like any other, our industry is going to continue to evolve as the tastes of our culture change. If you can anticipate the trends that are coming you'll be in a much better situation to stay nimble and consequently relevant. I'm going to give you a few ideas on how to position your club for success in the coming years based on what I've witnessed and experienced.

WHAT WILL STAY THE SAME

I have an optimistic outlook for what the next 10 years and beyond will bring for private clubs. At our very core, we are wired to connect and I believe there is no better way to do this than to form a group of like-minded individuals, a club. This is not something that's ever going to change.

Clubs also provide an outlet for competition, another core element to the human experience. Without competition, there is no progress because there's no desire to push yourself beyond the self-imposed boundaries we set. I think folks will continue to belong to and form clubs to pursue these activities.

Finally, there are young leaders in our industry who are poised to take up the mantle of leadership and of membership marketing who aren't afraid to embrace new trends or tackle new challenges. I think these folks will continue to push the boundaries of what's possible as an industry, and together, we'll find ways to remain relevant to our membership by providing new services, amenities and programming.

FUTURE TECHNOLOGY

I think technology will continue to develop and shape the member experience. As mobile apps and beacon technology evolves, I can see a time where more and more things will be automated and personalized. The app of the near future will also be more predictive. It will elevate the experience in a very personalized way.

Imagine this scenario: You walk into the club and your daily workout routine pops up on your phone. It tells you what machines to use, how much weight to lift and how much time you should spend.

Next you walk into the dining room. As you enter the room, the daily specials appear on the app. You also receive recommendations based on the specific diet you're on to achieve optimum health--whether that's a low-carb diet, a high-protein diet, gluten-free diet, etc.

Next you walk onto the tennis courts or golf course and you're matched with your playing partner for the day. Some information appears that tells you a little about them and what you have in common—where they come from, the university they attended, the business they're in, and the family they have.

At the end of your match, you receive a readout of your heart rate and the calories you've burned. The app will give you some suggestions for the upcoming events you would be interested in at the club.

This is where I see private club technology headed. More and more information will be stored to make the experience unique and extraordinary. I hope it comes sooner than later.

WHAT WILL CHANGE

I think there will be a big push back on communication technology from the millennial generation soon and that will benefit private clubs. This generation, of which I am one, is on the cusp of what came before and what's coming after. Millennials are wired in, but also burdened by it as well. I believe many in this generation feel that emails, calls, texts and notifications are getting out of hand. If clubs can be a haven to escape and unplug, I think they'll enjoy success. If you don't think they're capable of cutting the cord, just ask the cable television industry. It's different, but similar too.

Our world gets more dangerous each day. There are more and more mass shootings and massacres. Many of our private clubs are behind gates or have some form of building security. I think this will be a big motivator for families who are seeking safe environments.

Golf's role as the cornerstone of many of our private clubs will evolve. I don't see golf's shrinking market share amongst the general public as a bad thing. In fact, I think we're living in the age of the niche, and with golf becoming more niche, it will gain more prestige and value for those attracted to it. The more mainstream something is, the more it loses value. It's a weird quirk in our human perception. As golf becomes rarer, I think it will increase the perceived value of private club membership. I know it seems backwards but it has been proven over and over in other industries. It's the law of supply and demand at work. Clubs who market golf as a niche activity that will challenge you at your very core, will win.

I think by now we can see the writing on the wall when it comes to private clubs being a boys club. As clubs become more family friendly, they will be more desirable to the generations who are coming next. The clubs that are investing in fitness facilities, pool complexes, and children's programming are the ones that are winning and that will get exponentially more important in the coming years.

The last change I see coming is that branding and marketing will be embraced and this will be more widespread in the next 5 years. Simply by reading this book you have taken the first step in that direction. For too long our industry has been lurking in the shadows. It's time to come out and put it on display. There's greatness happening behind our walls. The smartest, most gracious and most talented people in our society are spending their time in, and working at our clubs. Let's tell that story together.

ABOUT THE AUTHOR

Gabriel Aluisy is the founder of The Private Club Agency, a Tampa, Florida based design, marketing and consulting firm focused on membership marketing and retention strategy at private clubs. He is the author of the bestselling book, **Moving Targets: Creating Engaging Brands in an On-Demand World** and the host of *Private Club Radio*, the industry's first and only weekly show dedicated to private club education.

Gabriel has been featured in *Entrepreneur*®, NBC, iHeart Radio, and many other leading publications. His keynotes have included the PCMA National Conference, The FLCMAA Club Summit, the Asia Pacific Golf Summit and many regional events. He is a graduate of American University's School of Communication.

Gabriel resides in Tampa, Florida with his wife, Ana, and two sons, Lucas and Marco. He's passionate about golf, tennis, travel, culture and automatic timepieces. Visit aluisy.com to learn more.

To book Gabriel Aluisy to speak at your next event:
Call 813-344-4769 or email gabe@privateclubagency.com

TUNE IN MONDAYS TO PRIVATE CLUB RADIO

GET THE BEST IN PRIVATE CLUB EDUCATION FROM THE
INDUSTRY'S TOP EXPERTS. AVAILABLE ON ITUNES,
STITCHER OR YOUR FAVORITE PODCAST APP.

PRIVATECLUBRADIO.COM

CPSIA information can be obtained
at www.ICGtesting.com
Printed in the USA
LVOW07*2352071117
555262LV00002B/3/P